I0135533

FROM DARKNESS TO LIGHT

Testimonies of Six Holocaust Survivors

Cherry
Orchard
Books

FROM DARKNESS TO LIGHT

Testimonies of Six Holocaust Survivors

Ronald J. Diller

Library of Congress Cataloging-in-Publication Data

Names: Diller, Ronald J., author.
Title: From darkness to light : testimony of six Holocaust Survivors / Ronald J. Diller.
Description: Boston : Academic Studies Press, 2020. | Includes bibliographical references.
Identifiers: LCCN 2020040202 (print) | LCCN 2020040203 (ebook) | ISBN 9781644695067 (paperback) | ISBN 9781644695074 (adobe pdf) | ISBN 9781644695081 (epub)
Subjects: LCSH: Holocaust, Jewish (1939-1945)--Biography. | Holocaust, Jewish (1939-1945)--Personal narratives. | Holocaust survivors--Israel--Biography.
Classification: LCC D804.195 .D55 2020 (print) | LCC D804.195 (ebook) | DDC 940.53/180922--dc23
LC record available at https://lccn.loc.gov/2020040202
LC ebook record available at https://lccn.loc.gov/2020040203

Copyright © 2020 Academic Studies Press
All rights reserved.

Book design by Lapiz Digital Services.
Cover design by Ivan Grave.

Publisher by Cherry Orchard Books, imprint of Academic Studies Press.
1577 Beacon St.
Brookline, MA 02446
press@academicstudiespress.com
www.academicstudiespress.com

This book is dedicated to the memory of my loving mother, Helen Diller, who gave me the inspiration to share the lives of these precious people, for the whole world and future generations to know their stories of strength and survival through the nightmare of the Holocaust.

THE HELEN DILLER FAMILY FOUNDATION

The Foundation supports UCSF and other educational institutions worldwide. One of Its most notable youth programs is called *tikkun olam*, or "repairing the world." The Awards provide $36,000 for each recipient to further their initiative or education. The Foundation also funds the Diller Teen Fellows program, an international leadership program for Jewish teens established in San Francisco in 1997. The program has 16 partnerships and 32 participating communities in the US, Europe, South America, South Africa and Australia.

Contents

Preface

The Holocaust survivors interviewed for this book had the courage and conviction to share the intimate accounts of the atrocities they witnessed and underwent, which words cannot adequately describe. As Winston Churchill said, "If you're going through hell, keep going." In the period of one of history's darkest hours, millions of Jews were subjected to the hell on earth that was the Holocaust. This book walks readers through the lives of six survivors, told in their own words, so the world can have first-hand knowledge of what happened.

Now in their eighties and nineties, they can still recall in detail their darkest memories. I collected and selected them through hours of personal interviews with them and their children, and presented them here, with as little interference as possible, to preserve their voices. Each story is told in their own words, so the world can have first-hand knowledge of what happened to these individuals. Amid immense pain and suffering, they managed to overcome every obstacle they encountered under the Nazi regime. When they were liberated, it was their dream to make aliya to Israel. They settled in the Holy Land as visionaries and pioneers to build the Jewish state, which itself was undergoing wars and difficult economic times. Their love for the Jewish homeland and their creation of families that embody children, grandchildren, and great-grandchildren nullified Hitler's aim to annihilate the Jews. This was their miracle.

In recent years there has been a huge spike in antisemitic attacks worldwide. The Anti-Defamation League (ADL) reported that in 2019 there were 2,107 antisemitic incidents throughout the US. This 12% increase from the 1,879 incidents recorded in 2018 marks the highest number on record since ADL began tracking antisemitic incidents in 1979. Such attacks include vandalism, arson, and the distribution of white supremacist propaganda at synagogues and other Jewish institutions.

In 2019, the Community Security Trust (CST) recorded 1,805 antisemitic incidents in the UK—the highest total ever recorded in a single calendar year. This is 7% higher than the 1,690 antisemitic incidents in 2018, making 2019 the fourth consecutive year in which the annual record has been broken. In France, according to police statistics, antisemitic acts rose by 74% in 2018. France's interior ministry accounted for a total of 687 antisemitic acts in 2019 compared to 541 in 2018, a 27% increase.

Antisemitism continues to rip society apart. We hope that this book will help to never forget or overlook the grim reality of the Holocaust, and be a step towards eradicating hatred in the world toward people based on the way they look or how they practice their religion.

These six survivors, like many others, underwent atrocities and injustices that still plague their lives today. Words could never accurately describe what happened to them during the Holocaust. And yet after their liberation, fighting to find their way to Israel from Europe and establish a new life in Israel with no income, many with no identify papers, in a new country that didn't have luxuries, they kept their heads high. Despite all, they never let Hitler kill their dreams to one day live in Israel, and for accomplishing this miracle "they won."

Foreword

Tragedy and Triumph: The Life and Legacy of Am Yisrael

Rabbi Stewart M. Weiss

Jewish life—it cannot be disputed nor avoided—is a mystical mixture of tragedy and triumph. These two physical and emotional poles of the human experience travel with us wherever we sojourn, and they form the backdrop for history's most compelling human story. Biblical heroes Avraham, Sarah and Yitzchak, despite their prominence on the world stage, had their Akeida to grapple with, while Yakov faced innumerable challenges throughout his own life, including the death of his beloved wife Rachel, the kidnapping and assumed death of his favorite son Yosef, and his descent into the depravity of Egypt.

Moshe, for his part, was not afraid to confront God regarding divine justice. He asked of Hashem, "*Hareini-na et k'vodecha*" (Show me Your glory), which the rabbis interpret as inquiring why Bnei Yisrael had to suffer so greatly before their eventual liberation.

Although at first glance this appears to be Moshe throwing up his hands in resignation, the rabbis interpret this statement very differently. Moshe, as the truest prophet, understood that he would not be the ultimate Redeemer. While he would indeed liberate the Israelites from Egypt, that would mark only the beginning of our struggle, not the end. We would go on to suffer countless catastrophes, such as expulsions from our Holy Land at the hands of the Babylonians and the Romans, pogroms, inquisitions, and the Holocaust. So, Moshe—ever the great defense attorney of the people of

Israel—argued passionately to the Almighty: "Please, God, send the final *Goel* now. Spare my people this endless parade of misfortunes!"

But Hashem was emphatic in His denial of Moshe's request, for the history of our nation is not one-dimensional; it is not limited exclusively to success and salvation. It is a series of both great victories and frightening dangers, a cosmic combination of the highest highs and the lowest lows. It is not a pattern that we would choose, perhaps, but it is ours to contend with nonetheless, until our final *Geula*.

The secret to Jewish survival, I contend, is two-fold: We must steel ourselves to somehow endure the pain and suffering we encounter—both as individuals and as a people; and we must discover how to turn the dark days into light, distilling hope and glory out of our deepest despair. Even at the very lowest moments in our lives, we must claw our way back to normalcy, back to our elite status as God's chosen first-born, reviving and rejuvenating our faith in both God and ourselves. And we must train ourselves to see God's hand in all things, acknowledging a higher plan and ultimate justice, despite that which we consider irredeemably unjust.

When Aaron the Kohen Gadol's sons Nadav and Avihu die, the Torah records his reaction as "*Va'yidom Aharon*"—Aaron was paralyzed, speechless, immobile. Most readers would assume that Aaron was simply too grief-stricken to respond. But Rabbi Moshe Feinstein offers a striking viewpoint. Nadav and Avihu, he says, were *tzadikim*, righteous people—indeed, even Moshe tells his brother, "They are more righteous than you and I!" But they overstepped their boundaries in a passionate desire to draw closer to Hashem, and they were taken. Aaron thus is caught between two diametrically opposed emotions. On the one hand, he is overwhelmed with sadness at the loss of his eldest sons, his heirs apparent. Yet at the same time, he is sent a vision that in the halls of Heaven, the angels are giving the grandest of welcomes to these two extraordinary individuals who have earned their exalted place in Gan Eden. And so, not knowing whether to cry out in pain or sing out in joy, Aaron does the only thing he *can* do he remains silent.

My wife Susie and I can fully relate to this scenario. Our eldest son, staff Sgt. Ari Yehoshua, served as a member of the IDF's Sayeret Nachal elite anti-terror unit. He was involved in countless dangerous missions during the second intifada. When his unit captured Hamas headquarters in Shechem (Nablus) in 2002, he was killed in a firefight between the Israeli army and the terrorists. He died while helping to save the life of a fellow soldier.

And so, while Susie and I mourn Ari's death every day of our lives, we also feel immense pride in his stature as a true hero of Israel and the Jewish People. His courage and ultimate self-sacrifice grant him an eternal place in the annals of our nation's epic struggle, and we stand in awe of his strength and stature.

Some years ago, I told the stirring story, in my column in *The Jerusalem Post*, of Chaim and Baruch Shapiro, a story that would ironically become our own personal narrative. Chaim had survived four concentration camps. During the Shoa, he lost his wife and seven of his children, without having the chance to even sit shiva for them. He was finally liberated from Buchenwald with his only surviving son, Baruch. They spent three years in a DP camp until finally, in 1948, they found place aboard an immigrant ship and came to Israel.

They landed in the midst of the War of Independence, with the fledgling nation fighting a desperate battle for survival against overwhelming odds. So, Baruch volunteered to fight. With no previous training, he was handed a rifle, taught how to shoot, and was sent off to war. Baruch distinguished himself in battle as part of the Harel Brigade, fighting to break the Arab siege of Jerusalem. He was even awarded a medal for bravery under fire.

Then, one day, Chaim received the bitter news that his son had been killed in battle. Chaim had only one request: he wanted his son to be buried in Jerusalem, on Mount Herzl, the national military cemetery. The next afternoon, hundreds of mourners gathered at Mount Herzl. Most of them had never known Baruch or his father, but they had heard of the tragedy and wanted to pay their respects. After all, what Hitler had not finished in the crematoria had ended with an Arab bullet. This was the last Shapiro son, the end of a line. Yigal Yadin, the IDF chief of staff, stood by Chaim Shapiro's side during the funeral.

As Baruch's coffin was being lowered into the ground, Chaim began to sing. People thought he had gone crazy from grief and tried to quiet him, but he shrugged them all off and continued singing. Finally, Chaim spoke:

> I have been through a hell the likes of which most people cannot imagine. I lost over 70 relatives in a little over a year, including seven children, my wife, and my parents. I have no place to mourn them, no grave. They are ashes in the skies over Europe, and I have no idea *why* they had to die. But *this* son, I

do know why he died. He died in glory, fighting as a proud soldier on behalf of the entire Jewish People, in defense of our own precious land and the State of Israel. His grave is not unmarked; it is in a place of honor on Mount Herzl in Jerusalem. And that is not a reason to cry, it is a reason to sing.

When Chaim finished speaking, he began to sing once again and to grab people's hands to dance. And so, as Baruch's flag-draped coffin was lowered into the ground, 300 mourners sang and danced against the setting sun of the Jerusalem sky.

Baruch and Chaim Shapiro's story is the story of our nation, our history. We undergo fierce trials, we are bloodied and wounded, but somehow, we survive. In fact, we flourish. We are the most resilient, determined and indestructible of any people to ever walk this Earth.

Am Yisrael chai.

Rabbi Weiss was educated at the Beit Midrash L'Torah (Hebrew Theological College) in Skokie, Illinois, where he received his degrees in Hebrew literature and rabbinical studies. He served as the rabbi of congregations in Chicago and Dallas and was head Jewish chaplain at Rush Medical Center in Chicago. He made aliya in 1992 and lives in Ra'anana, where he directs the Jewish Outreach Center. He is a regular columnist for The Jerusalem Post *and lectures frequently in Israel, the US, England, and South Africa.*

Chapter One

Christianity Saves my Life

Lilian Ronen

My name is Lilian Nissenbaum. I changed my last name to Ronen, my married name, when I made aliya to Israel. I was born in Warsaw, Poland, on August 17, 1931. My family was considered financially well off, and we grew up in an up upper-class environment. We lived in a four-room apartment at 13 Elektoraina Street. I had a brother, Victor (Vitech), who was three years younger than me. We had a maid and a nanny who lived with us.

My mother, Yocheved, changed her name to Julia, but we called her Juliet. She was a housewife, a very beautiful woman with black hair and dark brown eyes. She came from Lublin, Poland, from a poor family. I never knew her parents.

My father, Ephraim, changed his name to Alfred; but according to Polish records his birth name was Zelman. He had blue eyes and blond curly hair. His parents were Orthodox Jews from Lublin. All I remember about my paternal grandparents is that I was afraid of them because I was raised in a non-religious home. They lived in poverty and could not afford to raise my father, so they sent him to live with his aunt Sarah. While living in her home, he received a secular education.

My father was an engineer. He established a factory that produced cast concrete pavement slabs. He started the business with a Polish partner, but later he ran the business on his own. Life was good until the war started. My father was a member of the Bundism movement, a Jewish socialist organization in Eastern Europe that stood against Nazism. He felt Polish and resented being Jewish. My parents knew Yiddish, but they spoke

Polish at home. It was only on rare occasions when they didn't want us to understand them that they spoke Yiddish.

I attended an affluent private Jewish elementary school from kindergarten through to second grade. We were taught Hebrew. The school was located on the street where we lived.

I remember our family vacations. My parents rented a vacation home for two months in the town of Jozeoff. When we drove toward Jozeoff, near Otwock, my father never wanted to stop in Otwock because there were too many Jews! My mother stayed with us while Dad was at work in Warsaw, but he would join us from time to time.

In the winter, my father used to go skiing in the resort town of Zakopane. He promised me that when I turned ten, I could join him on the ski slopes.

In my early childhood, I was closer to my mother than to my father, but I loved him very much. I remember my mother's elegant dresses of the 1930s, with her matching scarves.

Almost every day, we children played in Saski Park in Warsaw under the supervision of our nanny. There was a certain bench in the playground that I vividly remember. Happy memories of my early childhood came flooding back when I saw that bench again fifty years later.

Saski Park, Warsaw, Poland.

My family chose not to observe most of the Jewish holidays, and we didn't go to synagogue. The only Jewish holidays we celebrated were Passover and Yom Kippur. For Passover, we had many gentiles join us for the Seder. My parents never fasted on Yom Kippur.

My younger aunt, Hanka, was a cheerful, warm, and beautiful woman. She was a very positive figure in my life.

My mother did not like jewelry, but my father liked to buy it for her. When I was a little girl, he bought me a gold ring and an enamel pin with pearls. Later, when economic times became tough, I sold the jewelry to survive. My father bought me a plot of land near Warsaw named after me in the town of Milosna.

Before the Warsaw Ghetto was formed, my aunt Hanka was a nurse at Umschlagplatz Hospital. She had a "fictitious" marriage to a Jewish doctor, thinking that this could protect her from the Nazis. My eldest aunt Esther was married to a policeman. After the war, I don't know what happened to them.

The war began on September 1, 1939. The Poles and the Jews were ill prepared. Bombs started to drop, but Poland had no air defense. The German planes flew so low that we could clearly see their swastikas. The sky was red with fire. One day at the beginning of the war, an order was issued that all the men had to leave Warsaw. My father went with the other men in a caravan, while the women and children were left alone.

The bombing went on for about a month. One time, a bomb landed on our porch, but fortunately it failed to explode. Before a bombardment, we'd go for cover to the basement of our building. If there was a fire in our building due to the bombing, we would flee to other apartment buildings. We endured a month of mad fires, panic, and destitution. We did not have food, as no one had prepared provisions in advance.

When the war broke out, my mother feared there would not be any bread, so she made jars of strawberry jam and packed up boxes of sardines. For weeks, we ate jam and sardines. During the onslaught of the fierce bombing, communication with others was cut off. It was utter chaos. After a month, my father returned home. We did not know where he had been or what he had gone through.

In the meantime, the Germans entered Warsaw with a grand procession that I will never forget. That was the formal beginning of the "Occupation." In the first phase, there was still a sense of solidarity among the neighbors. We lived in an area that was on the border of the Ghetto, a mixed area of

Jews and Christians. In the first month, everyone was busy with survival, with no prevalence of antisemitism.

No one could have imagined what the Germans were about to do. At the beginning of the Occupation, the Warsaw Ghetto was an open area. But by October 1940, the Nazis forced the Jews to live in the Ghetto. At that time, Jews were starting to come from the towns and villages surrounding Warsaw. The Germans insisted that we wear the armband with the white ribbon and blue Star of David. When the Ghetto was created, there were about 360,000 Jews in Warsaw. More than 200,000 Jews were concentrated within its borders. When the Ghetto closed on November 16, 1940, it had more than half a million Jews.

In October 1939, I was enrolled in a Polish school. After two weeks, the teacher said, "All the Jews, get up." Three of us stood up. He said, "I am very sorry to tell you, but the Germans do not allow you to study." That is how my education ended in Warsaw outside the Ghetto. Between October and November, it was still safe to play in the yard.

In every Polish building there was a guard. I became friendly with the guards and took them with me when I went to play in Saski Park, which was forbidden to Jews. No one knew I was Jewish.

The Germans confiscated my father's property, which included the land, factory, and machinery. The Germans used his concrete slabs to build an airport. Dad had investment securities at a Polish bank that lost all their value. He managed to save porcelain from his factory, which he hid in the basement and then sold some to make money. He found work in the *Judenrat* [Jewish council appointed by the Nazis within Jewish communities as a means to control them and ensure order in the ghettos]. That enabled us to get by and put food on the table.

While the Ghetto was operational, we were still living in our apartment. One day, some German soldiers came to our home and beat my father to demand money from him. It was shocking. We continued to live in our apartment, but I was so traumatized by that experience that I was vacillating between life and death. I contracted typhoid. Our doctor, a pediatrician, was a neighbor. He and my aunt Hanka secretly treated me at home to avoid sending me to a hospital. I heard that nobody came out of the hospital alive. If I had been sent to hospital, the building would have been quarantined for forty days. The doctor continued to treat me. At one point, I lost consciousness. Finally, after two months, I recovered. As part of my rehabilitation, I had to learn how to walk again. Nobody in my building knew about my illness, and no one else was infected.

In December 1940, the Polish government declared our street as territory belonging to the Ghetto. We left our apartment and handed everything over to the Poles. Two days later, as Dad was walking down the street, he saw a truck loaded with all our belongings.

We started wandering from apartment to apartment. Initially, we lived in a small apartment. But as more people moved into the Ghetto, it became crowded and we were forced to share our living quarters with other families.

Dad's work in the Judenrat gave us access to food to avoid being hungry, and we even managed to host Jewish children for lunch. Dad put away money, which enabled us to get by, while others were in much more dire situations.

During the early period in the Ghetto, I took a notebook to the teachers' houses. In secret, I learned arithmetic and French. I formed a group with two other girls, Mila and Janka. I managed to read many books. The three of us survived the war on the streets.

A few months after moving into the Ghetto, the three of us wandered through the streets, living as survivalists. We called ourselves "the street children." All day long we'd roam the streets in small groups, and our parents lost all control of our movements. In our apartments, people were living one on top of the other, so staying at home was not an option.

Long before the atrocities of the Ghetto began, the Judenrat in Warsaw, which oversaw the cemeteries, set up an organization called Toporol. It created jobs to keep children off the streets by having them cultivate gardens and grow vegetables.

As part of our job, we buried dead people who were brought to us from the streets. After a while, we became indifferent to death. There are no words to describe the horrors of what I saw and experienced. At first, the corpses were collected on wagons, but they couldn't keep pace with the vast number of bodies piling up. At one point, we stopped burying the dead bodies and just threw them into mass graves.

During that time, my mother became pregnant and aborted the baby. She thought I didn't know, but it was impossible to hide.

Mila and I ridiculed women who resorted to prostitution to earn money just to eat. My friend and I worked for the prostitutes on the street. They were decent women who had to become sex workers.

There was a thriving black market between the Jews and the Germans. One Jewish underground group was called Group 13. There was a theater and numerous cafes—a vibrant entertainment life.

The Judenrat levied taxes in certain areas of the Ghetto. My father was one of the men who oversaw this effort to collect tax payments from the Jews. Everyone paid what they could afford. It was unpleasant work, but it was a matter of survival. It meant that at times the Germans got into arguments with the Jews. When that job ended for my father because he was unsuccessful in collecting money, he became the guard of a building on Pawiak Street, opposite the Pawiak Prison, where many people were tortured.

The Ghetto took a turn for the worse on July 22, 1942. There were numerous homeless people, starvation, and countless beggars seeking handouts. The Germans promised us bread and jam.

The Ghetto was divided according to one's economic status. Broken down per person, it is summarized as follows:

- 20,000 lived comfortably
- 200,000 were *status quo*
- 250,000 lived in poverty and were expected to die of starvation

Umschlagplatz Hospital was evacuated and was turned into a deportation center for the Jews. The railroad tracks led to the hospital. For two days, Jews walked with the Germans in long convoys to Umschlagplatz Hospital. In the evening, the Nazis engaged in terror against the Jews. Jewish collaborators were killed, and the remaining survivors were then taken to Umschlagplatz Hospital.

As more and more people began to die, the Ghetto became smaller. Each time another street was wiped out, those who had not been taken away moved to other internal streets. People took to living on the streets. The Germans put them in a kind of triangle and took them to Umschlagplatz.

Those who survived had nowhere to go. Their homes were destroyed. Over time, streets that remained in the Ghetto were cut off from each other, creating artificial islands around small factories.

There were Jewish commandos whose job it was to transfer the vacated apartments to the Germans. The Ghetto became fragmented and broken up. Between the small and large sections was a wooden bridge that Jews traversed. The bridge served as a conduit for Jews inside the Ghetto, but it was later torn down. Within two months, normal life ceased and it became a constant struggle for survival.

In one of the apartments lived a family of Jews who had converted to Christianity three generations before. In one of the Germans' actions against the Jews, the family was taken away. A little canary in a cage was left on the windowsill, and it soon became a beloved pet of mine. A German soldier saw the birdcage from the street and came up to our apartment. He asked me whom the bird belonged to, and I said it was mine. He immediately took my little canary away.

In 1942, life in the Ghetto was becoming harder by the moment. We could no longer depend on food distributions from charitable organizations. Whenever the Germans initiated an action against the Jews in the Ghetto, we had to hide. The first such action started in July and lasted until August. One day, the Germans entered our apartment building and made the occupants stand in threes. In front of me stood Janusz Korczak with his children. When my father heard about this, he called his brother-in-law David, the Jewish police officer. Luckily, my uncle arrived and found us. He told the Germans that we were his family—his wife and children. So, we were saved again.

Now we couldn't go back to our apartment, so we moved in with our uncle for a short time. From there, we found other hiding places such as a bakery with double doors; rooms with hidden entrances; and basements whose upper entrances were covered with furniture or carpets.

By 1942, we heard about the Treblinka extermination camp from people who had fled and told us about their experiences. There were three days in September when German soldiers gathered in a certain square for the selection of the Jews. My father and twenty other people in our building decided that we should remain inside and hide in the basement which had a window facing the street. We remained in complete silence, hidden in two rooms that were used for singing songs and get-togethers. Babies were muffled to keep them quiet. For three days it was completely quiet, and we saw the Germans patrolling the street with barking dogs. We did not know what happened to all the Jews and what would happen to us. Suddenly, we heard banging on the floor above us. The Germans had found our hiding place. My father approached the Germans and bribed them with money to avoid our arrest.

After three days of sitting in silence, people began to return to their apartments. Returnees had special residence permits—licenses granted to essential workers (in factories, for example).

From that point on, those in the Ghetto who did not have proper papers had to live underground. The licenses would be changed intermittently to detect forged documents. Those who didn't have licenses didn't receive food. People without permits did not get even half a loaf of bread. Being illegal was a death sentence.

It was a harsh winter. There were only 60,000 Jews left in the Ghetto, whereas at the start of the war in 1939 there were half a million. We didn't know how to deal with the sights of poverty and death on the streets because we didn't know what to expect. I was only twelve years old. The harsh circumstances matured me like an adult, and that scared me.

We were living in an apartment in the building on Pawiak Street where my father worked as a guard. The people who had lived in the building had been deported, and it was now occupied by Germans and doctors. The Germans let us live there because my father was the guard. My brother and I spent most of our free time reading. We were constantly looking for books. The abandoned apartments were furnished, and some even had dinner plates on the tables. We wandered around the apartments looking for books and other treasures.

On February 26, 1943, I left the Ghetto and was taken into a room at Umschlagplatz Hospital. Dad left us and said that he was going to look for a way for us to be saved. At one point, the Germans entered our room and started shooting like madmen. It was terrible. By sheer luck, nothing happened to us.

Towards evening, we were taken out of the building to a ramp of railway cars. We took our time, refusing to walk fast. The rampage was indescribable. Jewish policemen were beaten. That is a black spot that will always haunt Warsaw Jewry. It was the worst day of my life. Every time the lines moved forward, we moved backward. Ultimately, our turn came. It was dusk and Dad, who had left in the morning, was not with us during this chaos. The Germans were forcing people onto the railway cars. My mother said to us, "Let's walk back three steps each time," and that is what we did. We were the last in the group.

The Germans were walking back and forth, monitoring the lines with their dogs. Next to us stood three young men, and behind them was a wall. We stood on the embankment between the railway cars. People began to run, slipping into the doorway between two walls behind another wooden wall. My brother saw people uproot a few slats from the wall. He managed to slip through the space and started running. My mother and I followed him, and we ran to the nearest street.

My mother, who did not lose her resourcefulness, said, "Give me your hands and be quiet." We didn't know if we were still in the Ghetto or on a street outside the Ghetto. When we passed through the doorway, we walked a few meters and came to another corner. Ten steps past the door, we encountered a German patrol walking indifferently as if nothing was happening.

The German patrol saw the break in the wall and started firing rapidly. We were terrified but were able to get to the next alley, evading the soldiers. We found ourselves in one of the islands in the Ghetto where Germans stockpiled clothing from abandoned property that was shipped to Germany. For some reason, the Germans welcomed us and let us eat and drink. We were illegals on the run with no documents.

I decided to explore the streets after curfew to look for my father. I knew that he had hidden a stash of money in our old apartment. I went to the apartment at night to see if the money was there—a sign that Dad was alive. After searching for us for a few days, my father found us.

The Jewish commando hid and fed us, knowing that we did not have permits. The commandos lived on the left side of the street. On the other side there were no Jews, and the apartments were empty. One day, the Germans came looking for Jews. The Jewish commandos moved us to the other side of the street, where we hid in one of the empty apartments under the bed linen. My mother, Vitek, and I were hiding in one place, and I cannot remember where Dad was at that time. The Germans entered the apartment and began to stab the quilt with bayonets. Miraculously, we survived.

In February 1943, my father contacted Zusia, the widow of a Polish friend of his from university. A woman in her thirties with a young daughter, she agreed to let us stay with her. We left the Ghetto hidden among a group of Jews who went to work on the Polish side. My father paid the head of the group, who was a German or Polish policeman.

Once we got to the Polish side, my father pulled me out of the group, and we ran to Zusia's house. My father gave Zusia money and some jewelry. We slept there that night and returned to the Ghetto the next day with the same group of workers.

I said goodbye to my father and stayed with Zusia. It was dangerous for me to be there because the guards were usually informers for the Germans. Despite the danger, I lived with Zusia for about two months. If anyone asked who I was, I was introduced as Zusia's cousin or some such fabrication.

In April 1943, the Jewish uprising broke out in the Warsaw Ghetto. The sky was red from incineration. A few days after the uprising, I received a call from my father. He asked me to meet him in the Ghetto, at the spot where met to go to Zusia's. Before arriving, he instructed me to say to the German/ Polish policeman at the entrance "I'm a Jew and I owe you money"—only to avoid problems. I don't think there were more than fifty people in the Ghetto. The policeman touched my arm like a mezuzah.

Once I passed the entrance, I saw my father, but I almost couldn't recognize him. He suddenly looked like an old man with white hair. I was the first and only person to enter the Ghetto after the uprising. A man gave me some money. It's not clear where he was from. He didn't tell me what he did in the uprising, if he was fighting or not, but I think he was one of the rebels.

The meeting with my father was brief, and I knew he had nowhere to go. That was my last fifteen minutes with him. I don't remember being scared. I learned that my brother had been taken to the Poniatow concentration camp and that my mother had been killed on the first day of the Ghetto uprising.

The guards in the Polish apartment buildings were informers, so every time an apartment had to be registered at the Interior Ministry and one had to obtain all documentation of ownership. My father gave me a fake certificate of poor quality. It said that I was born in Lvov in the Ukraine. Authentic birth certificates were written in Latin, but mine was written in Polish. My new name was Oz Khovska.

I created a new identity for myself. I said I was an orphan from a very poor family. Zusia told the guard that I was a distant relative—a refugee from the east. There were a lot of refugees from the Ukraine.

One day, a postcard arrived from my father. He was living in the tiny village of Kashyunsh, near Majdanek, which can barely be found on the map. He asked me to send him a package of food. I bought the food and sent the parcel to the address that appeared on the postcard. He may have been hiding in a Polish home or joined the partisans because the village was in a forest area where many partisans operated. I didn't hear from him anymore. There had been a recent shipment of Jews from the Ghetto to

Majdanek. My father's life may have ended in the Majdanek extermination camp. That postcard was his last sign of life.

I was alone and wandering around, thinking about the Catholic religion. Near Zusia's apartment lived a Polish woman with a daughter my age who looked Jewish. The woman was blonde and looked German. I did a lot of housework for her and took care of her daughter. I cleaned the hardwood floor with large bars of soap. I was living and hiding on the Polish side of the Ghetto for seven years while not attending school.

The guard of Zusia's building apparently knew there was a Jew living there. The Germans came in one night when I was sleeping and lit up my face with a flashlight to see what I looked like. Then they went into the apartment next door and took the girl. They released her, thanks to her mother's connections, but I could not stay with Zusia from that moment on. Zusia gave me some money and the little bit of jewelry that Dad had left her and called her cousin for help. They hid my jewelry in a closet in a room where a prostitute worked. I sat in the closet for about two weeks in the dark, but I saw and heard nothing. Then she got sick of me and sent me away.

I moved in with Zusia's relatives on the Polish side of town. Her cousin brewed vodka from potatoes. It was illegal, but the business flourished. The family let me sleep on an old mattress at night; but in the morning, before the landlady woke up, I had to leave.

From six o'clock in the morning I started wandering the streets until seven p.m. After the curfew, the cousin would meet me on the street and take me back to the house. This went on for several months. In the morning he would give me money for a bun. It was cold, and I only had a thin raincoat. Luckily, the police didn't stop me because I looked like a beggar.

I lived under terrible hygienic conditions. In the mornings, I went to a Polish church with an elderly Polish woman. It was mainly to warm up, but at the same time I attended morning mass. The church was my shelter to keep me out of the rain and cold. To pass the time, I began to attend Catholic funerals. I chose not to go downtown where there were informers and blackmailers, making it too dangerous. I often spent time in the beautiful Powazki Cemetery gathering chestnuts from the trees.

Slowly I found solace in the Catholic religion. I became attracted to Catholicism for its rituals and symbols. I was practically agnostic. Although I was Jewish, religion didn't play a part in my life. When I was thirteen, I noticed a change. In the building where I was living, tenants gathered in the yard at seven in the evening to sing liturgical songs next to a makeshift statue of Mary. I learned all the songs. Zusia took me to a church that was in Three Crosses Square. She taught me basic prayers in case I was caught and had to prove I was a Christian. I began to believe in Jesus, Mary, and the stories of the saints; but inside, I always knew I was Jewish. I never went to confession. Perhaps that was due to my basic Jewish upbringing.

Zusia's mother, who helped me find refuge with her relative, chose not to roam the streets with me. I was a vagabond without a home, alone with no permit papers. Sometimes people on Moshe Street would stop and give me a sandwich or some money. I hung out with Zusia so I wouldn't be alone. She risked her life to help me.

Zusia introduced me to a woman who took me with her long distances on trains. In the freezing cold, we'd travel up to Minsk to buy geese, ducks, and chickens on the black market. As we passed the remote Polish villages, we would see snow that was knee deep. We bought birds, put them in a coat, and smuggled them to Warsaw. One time we walked up the mountains in the snow, passing through miles of villages in minus-thirty-degree weather without food or warm clothing.

One day, Zusia came to me and cried. She gave me fifty zlotys and said, "I can't do anything for you anymore." And that is when she left me.

I decided to turn myself over to the Gestapo. I was tired, malnourished and had no shelter. I just wanted to put an end to my story. As was I walking toward the Gestapo headquarters, I looked up and saw a sign that read "RGO." It was a government-approved voluntary social welfare organization that handled Polish refugees. I was dirty, dressed in rags, and in an overall terrible condition.

When the people at RGO saw my bedraggled condition, they took me straight to the manager. She immediately realized I was Jewish, which I didn't deny. She sent me to a transit center that had a first-aid station where people slept on stretchers. Zusia had warned me not to talk to anyone. When I arrived there, I became sick and lost consciousness, but I later recovered. The fifty zlotys that were in my pocket were gone.

When I got back on my feet, a woman named Hannah took me to a shelter to stay for a few nights. In the shelter, there were beggars and disabled people. I slept on a table. I saw the corpses of alcoholics.

The manager of the RGO employment office found me a job as a housekeeper and caretaker of two children and their grandmother. I was touched by their kindness, and my being Jewish was not a factor. But the payment was too meager, so I had to find new work. I went back to the Home Office to get a new ID and change my address. That was a nightmare.

I found a new residence and a new job at a nearby bakery, selling bread. That was the start of my brief commercial career. I began work at sun-up, buying rolls and selling them on the street, to private homes and to businesses. I gave my earnings to the Polish family I was staying with, who really loved me. One day, the owner of the bakery started investigating me, asking questions about where I was from to see if I was Jewish. They became suspicious of me, and their instincts told them I was Jewish. Naturally, I denied it.

One morning while selling bread, a band of hooligans, blackmailers, surrounded me and started screaming that I was a dirty Jew. I ignored them and continued to sell bread. They secretly followed me to see where I lived. One day when I returned from selling bread, the grandmother of the family, Maria, called me into her room. She said that the blackmailing hooligans had come to the house with guns, told her I was Jewish and asked for 500 zlotys. I finally had to tell her the truth, that I was Jewish. She cried because she loved me and said, "You have to leave." That put me in a very precarious position because I still hadn't received my new identity papers.

I continued my journey, looking for work as a housekeeper. I was hired by a family who lived in a beautiful home on Kisshikuna Street in Warsaw, where there were many palatial residences. The couple had eight children and a large domestic staff. They hired me to take care of the kids and work in the kitchen as a cook's assistant. I peeled apples. To enter the home, I had to pass through a gate guarded by a German guard and present proof with a certificate of residence. So, I had to inform the authorities of my new address. I managed to convince them to give me a passport.

There were other maids and caregivers, among them a beautiful eighteen-year-old girl. She liked me very much and tried to get me to go out on the town with her. After a while, I regained confidence, and we went into the city. When I returned to the house, the guard at the gate asked me for my personal documents, looked at my birth certificate and said I needed an ID. My friend said to wait for her, and she'd go with me to the Gestapo offices to get me an ID card. Five minutes later, she came out of the house and said to me, "What are you doing here?"—she started flirting with the German guard, made a date with him, and he let me go. All to distract the guard and protect me from him.

After that fiasco, the family fired me. I went to the manager of the employment office to tell her the news and ask her to find me a new job.

My next job was taking care of the infant of a young couple. The mother's name was Shelley. It was October 1944, the eve of the uprising in the Warsaw Ghetto. The couple hired me to accompany them on vacation to the town of Kazimierz near Warsaw. That is what saved me. When the uprising broke out, the German soldiers went from house to house to expel everyone until Warsaw was destroyed.

As we could not return to Warsaw, we were stuck in the village with no money, no place to go, and nothing to eat. Of course, the couple fired me.

I walked around the town and made friends with a local family. When I told them I had been fired, they invited me to their home. They fell in love with me and asked me to move in with them. They lived on a half-acre of land. I helped them graze cows and raise geese. They thought I worked for them exclusively, but that was not the case. Always in the forefront of my thoughts was that I was an illegal Jewish refugee trying to survive and feared death. In my spare time, I taught young children to read and write. I opened an informal school. I stayed in Kazimierz until the end of the war.

In January of 1945, German convoys entered the village of Kazimierz. At the end of the long street, we saw the Russians following in their footsteps. I was present during the battle between the Russians and the Germans. The Russians prevailed. In that battle, many mules were killed. The people from the village took the carcasses of the dead mules to feed the hungry. The Russians took over Kazimierz, absconded with the vodka, and wanted to rape the women who were in hiding, cowering with fear. The war was over. In the town, the farmers still wanted to adopt me. I wanted to return to Warsaw, but I didn't have any money.

I left and started to make my way to Warsaw to look for Zusia. After a few days of walking, I arrived in Warsaw, and my heart sank. The entire city was devastated. On ruined walls I found inscriptions of people who had found temporary shelter. I got to Zusia's house, but it was burned to the ground. I realized that I had nowhere to go. I had no place to sleep and no food to eat.

Then I met a man who asked me what I was doing. I told him I was alone and that I had nowhere to go. Warsaw was divided: one side was Poland and across the Vistula River was Prague in the Czech Republic. The man said he was on his way to Prague. He told me to go to a convent in Prague, where he knew someone. He wrote me a note and promised that they would take care of me there. He was right. The nuns accepted me without ever thinking that I could be Jewish.

Lili, 1946. Zakopane, Poland.

On my first morning at the convent, I had a pastry and a glass of juice, which stuck in my throat. I had been living on so few calories for so long that my body was weak and wasn't used to ingesting food. And I was suffering severely from lice. The insidious insects penetrated the seams of my clothes, and I always felt them on my skin and scalp.

I really wanted to study, so I asked the nuns if I could go straight into high school. I was able to study until the second month of grade two, then went directly into high school. I became an excellent student. I studied with great passion. When the other pupils would go out to dump the garbage, I'd follow them to get food.

One day on my way to school, I saw the sign of the Jewish Committee House. Jews were beginning to return to Warsaw, and I could see them sitting on the doorstep of the Committee House looking miserable and destitute. The last thing I wanted was for anybody to know my real identity as a Jew. However, I walked up to the entrance and approached the clerk. I said I was Jewish and asked for bread. He refused and told me to leave. I walked back down the stairs and cried.

Walking in front of me on the stairs was the head of the Jewish Committee. When he saw me, he immediately recognized me. It was Mr. Koschub, the father of a childhood friend of mine. He had survived with his entire family. He was in shock. The last time we had seen each other was in the Ghetto. He immediately went to the clerk, demanded that he give me a loaf of bread, and escorted me back to the convent. On the way there, he told me that I should leave the convent. I responded that I didn't want to be Jewish and that I had nothing in common with Jews. He was a smart man and said that he'd take me to a children's home in Zakopane for Jewish orphans. The resort town of Zakopane is in southern Poland, at the base of the Tatras Mountains. It's a popular destination for winter sports and summertime mountain climbing and hiking. The town is also known for its turn-of-the-twentieth-century wooden chalets, symbols of Zakopane-style architecture. Mr. Koschub told me to go to the convent and tell the nuns that he was a relative and that he'd bring me back to school and the convent in September. They made him promise that if I was unhappy for any reason, he'd bring me back sooner. He agreed.

Before our departure, I had two important accidental meetings. Firstly, I met a man my parents knew from the Ghetto, who told me he was with my brother on a train that led to the Poniatow concentration camp. He cried, and refused to tell me what happened to my brother. The man, who had survived the horrific experiences in Nazi Germany, didn't have the heart to tell me what he knew. He then disappeared, and to this day I do not know what tragic end my brother had—did he die from thirst on that train?

The other man I spoke with was my father's friend from the Ghetto. He told me that he saved his daughter and promised them a train ticket to Zakopane to be with them. I was treated as if I was his daughter.

During this period, I also went to the Jewish Committee to undergo a medical examination. Then I drove to Krakow to the Jewish Committee House at 38 Dulga Street. I stayed there for quite a while. This was the place where Jewish survivors from eastern Poland came—a sort of makeshift children's home. We were all in the same miserable situation. We wandered the streets all day, eating meager meals of soup and bread. The head of the Warsaw Council wanted me to leave the convent and bring me back to Judaism. But I didn't suffer in the convent. I lived there for many months and went to church.

Mr. Koschub indeed came to the convent to take me to the children's home. I was among the first group that went to Zakopane. It was paradise! Lena Küchler founded the home. She was a revered figure in my eyes. At our first meeting, she asked me questions about my family such as where I came from and what I went through during the war. I told her that I believed in the Catholic religion and asked to have a cross and pictures of the saints over my bed.

Lili in 1945. Zakopane, Poland.

Lena Kirschler.

Lena decided to send me to school outside the children's home. I went to the city's school called Szarotka, which in the Polish word for "edelweiss." I made up a story and told them that I lived in a Jewish children's home because my aunt was a cook, even though I was Catholic. Lena knew about what I said and did not object. I told her that I would not go to school as a Jew. She said, "You must attend school."

I didn't make any friends at that school. I had a great passion for learning. That is what interested me—learning and wallowing in books. But

I had a wonderful time at the children's home. It had a great atmosphere. Despite my opposition to the Jewish cause, I fit in well.

On Yom Kippur, when everyone was fasting, I sat alone in the dining room and ate an egg. Lena was tolerant and completely understood my situation.

When the summer was over, I chose to continue to stay at the children's home. I had made good friends there. I was elected head of the children's committee and became a judge. Many children in the house couldn't stand my cross and saints' pictures. But I was not the only one there who believed in Christianity, which was very important to me. My closest friends at the home were Nellie, Edith, and Dora. I had another friend, Siji, and a male friend, Janusz. Others enjoyed the children's home as well, such as Dana, Rouge, and Nathan. The whole story about the Children's Home can be seen in the film *Lena: My 100 Children*. I was one of the 100 displaced children taken from the Ghetto.

In the winter of 1946, there was a violent antisemitic attack on the children's home by the local militia. That is when I left for Lodz: I received a letter from a friend whose family name was Komorowski, promising me a train ticket to Lodz. I said goodbye to everyone at the children's home and registered my new family name as Komorowski.

In Lodz, I attended a private school for girls. That was one of the most memorable periods of my life. I was getting older and became interested in men.

I had many warm and loving friends. The Komorowskis decided to leave Poland and asked me if I wanted to stay or to go with them. They said they had relatives in France and could arrange official travel documents for me. They said they would register me as their daughter. I opted to join them.

In January 1947, we left Poland. For a short time, we lived in Grenoble, and then we moved to Paris. The Komorowski family's financial situation deteriorated rapidly, and they could barely make ends meet. I attended a Polish school in Paris. It was French during the time of Napoleon but after the war, the communists took over and it belonged to the Polish Embassy. I did my matriculation exams in Polish, which allowed me to be admitted to a French university without taking further exams. At the school, no one knew I was Jewish. My adoptive family was secular and assimilated and didn't want me to revert back to Judaism. My family name was Komorowski, so I was considered Polish. I obtained a Polish passport. I was an instructor at camps, aspiring to continue high school and obtain a university degree.

Due to the family's difficult financial situation, it became clear to me that after four years of my living with them, they were not able to continue to support me. At that time, Polish citizens were starting to return to university in Poland, and I was already one foot on the way there. The Komorowskis did not encourage me to return to Poland.

In the meantime, through the consulate, I received a one-year university scholarship to the Sorbonne from the Polish Students Organization. There was a course in psychometrics. When the head of the organization saw my certificate of excellence, he offered to register me directly for the second year. But I didn't meet the requirements. French was not my mother tongue. Out of 250 students, only twelve passed the exams, and I was not among them.

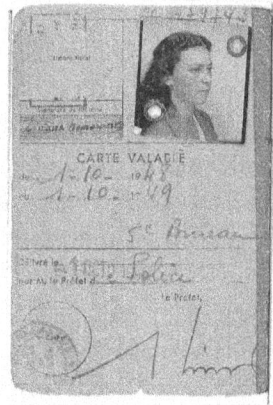

Polish and French Identification cards.

Lili, 18 years old. Sorbonne University, France.

During that year, I found work ironing clothes in the homes of French families. This gave me financial independence. However, at the end of the year I was in serious trouble.

I knew a Jewish man named Philip who worked in film and was active in organizing Jewish students. He knew I was Jewish and saw that I was Polish. He organized a trip to Israel. It was the first trip of Jewish students from France to Israel. Philip invited me to join the group. We set sail, and I fell in love with the State of Israel.

In Israel, my first visit was to Lena Küchler's house. I was enthusiastic about everything. Through the French government, I was introduced to the Ankelevich family, who owned a flower shop in Tel Aviv. They had lost a son in the War of Independence, and their daughter Rachel was eight years old. They were wonderful people and invited me to live with them. I wanted to be independent so I could study Hebrew in Jerusalem and enlist in the army.

I studied at Etzion Studio in Jerusalem. From there, I went straight into the army. I was twenty years old. I served at the Institute of Psychometric Diagnostics, thanks to my diploma and studies at the Sorbonne.

In the IDF, I was ranked as First Private Lillian Komorowski Nissenbaum. The camp where I was stationed was an open camp, but I needed a home. I went back to the Ankelevich family. Rachel welcomed me like a sister. It was a very generous offer. Miriam Ankelevich was a devout woman. She died at the age of forty-five. She never got over her son's death. I loved her dearly and mourned her throughout my life.

I was introduced to Rimon, my future husband, through a friend from Haifa. We met at the beach in Bat Yam where Rimon was a lifeguard. I visited him in Haifa, and he came to Tel Aviv. Rimon had immigrated to Israel from Budapest, Hungary at the age of fourteen. He came from a traditional Jewish family. His father worked as a publicist and journalist.

Lili, 19-year-old soldier in the IDF—just made Aliyah.

Lili and Rimon, 1952.

In March of 1953, after six months of dating, Rimon and I were married in Haifa at Yarmon Beach Carmel. We purchased a small apartment in the West Carmel neighborhood. The toilets and showers were outside. The next apartment we bought in Haifa was in Ramat Shaul. We financed the purchase by selling Rimon's camera and my flatware from France. Rimon worked in customs clearance, and I worked as a kindergarten assistant.

Our first son, Eitan, was born on February 25, 1957. On April 19, 1961 (the anniversary of my mother's death), our twins Orit and Dani were born, a month ahead of time.

Our beginning was difficult. In October of 1961, Rimon began working for ZIM in a high-level position. My husband was assigned to do overseas missions on behalf of the Israeli navy. It was financially rewarding and put us on our feet.

We lived in Eilat for five years. Then we moved to Belgium for eight years. In Belgium, our son Eitan suffered severely from asthma. The doctor said that he would have to live on cortisone for the rest of his life. I found another solution without medicine: we found Eitan a place to stay at a children's home in the Pyrenees at a high elevation in the mountains where the air was dry. He was only eight when we left him for four years with just a dictionary!

Rimon wanted to bring Eitan back to live with us, but I wanted to cure his asthma. We were living in Antwerp and traveled 1,500 kilometers to visit him. We visited our son on birthdays and spent two summer months with him in a rented apartment. After his four-year stay, he needed a year of psychological treatment to overcome his anger that his parents had abandoned him. Today, Eitan understands the difficult decisions we made and has never had to use cortisone.

Rimon continued to work in Belgium for another year, and I returned to Eilat with the children. After the twins enlisted in the army, I joined Rimon in Belgium. From there, we moved to Italy for five years. Then Rimon was assigned to Hong Kong, where we lived for six years. Hong Kong was one big paradise. I knew interesting people, and we lived a fascinating life, like overseas embassy officials.

Our children grew up and have families of their own. Eitan and Orit each have two sons. Our son Dani has two girls and a boy.

Lena with her family.

A Dedication to Lena Küchler-Silberman

Lena Küchler was born in Poland in 1910 in the town of Wieliczka near Krakow. She survived the Holocaust due to her tenacity to live and her love of children, whether Jews or non-Jews. She evaded the Gestapo, jumped from a train that was heading to the Blatzek death camp, and smuggled children from the Warsaw Ghetto and Krakow to save their lives. She worked as a caregiver for the Polish children.

At the outbreak of the war, she lived in Bosco, Poland. She wanted to return to her hometown to be with her ailing father. She worked in sewing factories set up by the Germans. From there, she moved to Russian-controlled Lvov.

After the German invasion in June 1941, she, along with the rest of the Jews of Lvov, were brought into the local ghetto. With forged papers, she fled from Lvov and returned to her father in Wieliczka. She worked as a teacher with her sister Pela until the demolition of the town by the Germans.

Lena arrived in Warsaw. Under the false name of Leontina Blitz, she worked in a German factory on the Polish side of town. There, she began to smuggle young children from the Warsaw Ghetto to the Polish side and place them in convents and monasteries.

After the defeat, she returned to the convents and monasteries to take the children away. That too came to an end. With the help of Polish friends, she received false papers and worked as a childcare worker in the town of Olkhovek, where she remained until the end of the war.

Lena with children in Zakopane, Poland.

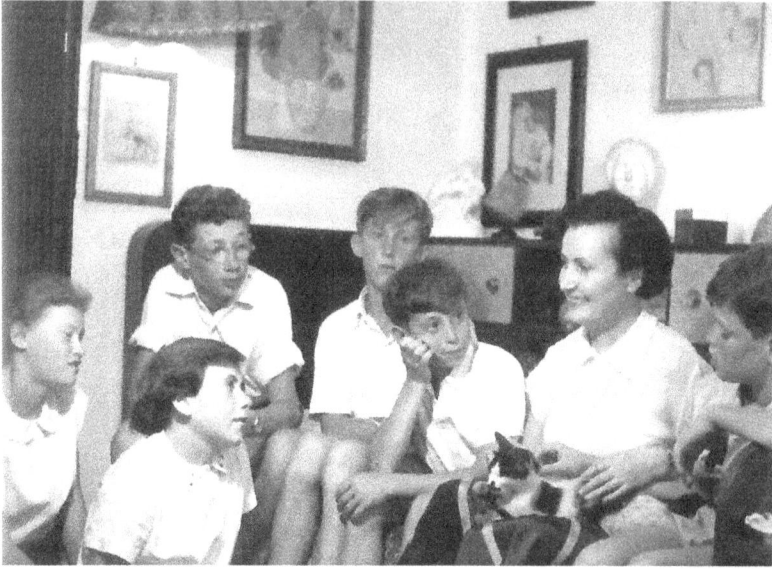

Lena with young children in Zakopane, Poland.

Lena with older children in Zakopane, Poland.

Lili in Zakopane, second to the right, 14-15 years old, with partisans.

One of the problems Lena dealt with was the assimilation of Jewish children. Many orphaned children, usually hungry and craving a warm bed, found their way into Catholic convents, monasteries, and churches across Poland. In war and famine, people would sell their souls for a warm bed and a loaf of bread.

About two months after the war was over, Lena arrived in Krakow. One day, she arrived at the Jewish Council on Duluga Street. Jewish survivors were searching for families, and she saw many orphaned children. That is when she decided to build a home for them.

She gathered 100 children and took them to Zakopane in the Carpathian Mountains, where she built a home for them. She had to work hard to raise money for donations from all kinds of Polish institutions and the JOINT. Lena, who was a great teacher, provided the children with food, clothing, and education.

The children, some of whom she had removed from convents or monasteries, she brought back to recognizing their Judaism. It was not easy to do after the horrors of war and ghetto life they had experienced. Many of the children lacked the initiative to try again, and some didn't remember that they were Jewish. Their Jewish identities were discovered by mere coincidence. The nuns and monks did their work for humane reasons, but their ultimate goal was to covert the children to Christianity.

The children who remained orphaned at such a young age had suffered from cold and hunger for four or five years. Suddenly they were welcomed into the arms of the church with its radiant lights and wood-burning heat, the scent of spices, and nourishing meals. They got used to this very quickly and were afraid of trying to live in new places. With all this, Lena had to fight, persuade, secure, all without financial support but with a tremendous amount of resourcefulness and dedication.

She later smuggled the children into France. Afterwards, she brought the 100 children to Israel, most of them to the Schiller Group kibbutz.

Lena took in children who roamed the streets in the Warsaw Ghetto, convents, monasteries, and charitable organizations. The JOINT (American Jewish Joint Distribution Committee,) gave bread rolls to the hungry children. Lena was able to save children from their death by giving them a new life.

I, too, benefited from Lena's selfless activities and created a home in Israel with my husband and three children and seven grandchildren. It will be a blessed memory.

Chapter Two

Salvation: Like a Needle in a Haystack

Miriam Wadislavki

My name is Miriam Greenshepoon, now Wadislavki. I was born on May 15, 1930, in a small town that was once in Poland called Warkowicze.

My brother Pinchas (Pinilla) was born two years after me. My father, Zvi Hershel Greenshepoon, was born in Wadislavki in 1898. My grandfather, Mottel Greenshepoon, was a rabbi, He was a wealthy man who owned forests and land. My grandmother Henia was the breadwinner in the family. She made an income granting small loans to the people in the town and the surrounding area. I still remember the two dressers in our house. In one dresser, there were drawers with bills she received from borrowers, all decorated with paintings. Yiddish was our mother tongue, but I also spoke Russian and Polish.

My father inherited forests and farmland from his father, which he leased to Czech farmers. My father worked in the grain trade, some of which he would receive from farmers as leasing fees. A gentile Czech man planted seeds to grow wheat. When there was a harvest, he would take bags of wheat by horse and carriage to sell in the nearby city of Rovno. Before he left at sunrise, my father would go to the synagogue to pray. We had a big grain warehouse, and from time to time my father would go out in the early morning in a grain-loaded wagon to trade with his customers. Whenever he returned from his travels, he would bring us chocolate, which he called Suchard.

My mother, Batya, was born in the Ukrainian town of Peredil, located ten kilometers from Warkowicze. Hers was the only Jewish family in the town. They kept potatoes, radishes, and cabbage in small jars. They had a beautiful flower garden near the house. Every summer, I'd go with my family to visit our relatives there. On one of the vacations, I went to the town of Sartan, where my uncle Nutta and Aunt Leah (Dad's sister) lived. Leah had a special room in the house with merchandise and cloth. She offered to make me a dress and let me choose the fabric. The dress, which had little flowers, was made from a fabric that did not require ironing.

We lived in a big house in the center of Warkowicze, which my grandfather built. It was so large that we rented rooms to another Jewish family. On the left side of the garden there was a tree with purple flowers, and on the right, there was a large cherry tree. We had a big yard with a horse cart, a chicken coop, and geese. We would bring the geese to the slaughterer, and we'd fry the fat in a large pot to make schmaltz for Passover and cabbage stuffed with meat. My mother made jams, which she stored in the basement. On the Jewish holidays, I'd give some jam to the rabbi who lived on our street.

The town had two synagogues. My father was a Cohen, and he prayed at the smaller synagogue. The larger one was called the Great Synagogue and had a beit midrash. In honor of Rosh Hashana, our Czech neighbors would give us honey. For the holiday, we would make a round honey cake. We also made a round challah with a "finger" pointing to the sky. On Simchat Torah, we ate red sugar-coated apples, which we speared into a flag with a lit candle on top. On Tu Bishvat, we received a package of dried fruits, which we were told were grown in Israel.

We never cooked on Shabbat—only on Friday. My brother would carry home two buckets of well water over his shoulder. Shabbat was a special time for our family. We all ate together and went to synagogue. We cooked in an open area with an oven that used wood which we called "prepature." For Friday night dinner and Shabbat lunch, my mother and grandmother made chicken soup with noodles, as well as carp that we bought at the market.

In our town there was a Jewish woman who married a gentile. The couple owned a café, but few people would go to their café because intermarriage among Orthodox Jews was taboo.

I had a Polish friend named Marusha when I was eleven years old. She invited me to her house to celebrate Christmas and help put the ornaments on the large fir tree. My grandmother was adamantly against this. With my other good friends from school, we'd go on hikes in the forest near the end of town and pick cranberries and blueberries. We also gathered chestnuts and pine nuts from the trees. There were two pools in the forest. In the winter, we would glide on the ice of the frozen pool with sleds and skis that my father made. On Saturdays and Jewish holidays, Jewish families would take strolls in the forest with their children, and young couples took leisurely walks. The Zionist youth movements had Lag Ba'Omer bonfires there and held special field days throughout the year.

My mother's parents died before the war. My mother married and moved to Warkowicze. My three uncles were married. The family members that remained were my grandmother Henia, my parents, my uncle Avraham (my father's younger brother), and my brother Pinchas. When my uncle Avraham married before the outbreak of the war, he built a house for his new family. My mother's sister Raziel stayed in Peredil with her husband Samuel Danai and their two children, Yankel and Rachel.

When I was six years old, my mother and grandmother said I needed to learn *lashon kodesh,* Hebrew. I studied with many of the children at the Jewish school in the Great Synagogue. When I was four, I studied with Rabbi Yitzhak Gross. He would come to our house in the afternoon to give me private lessons in Hebrew and Yiddish. When I was six, I was sent to study at the Polish school, where I studied until I was nine. I was the only student in my class who received a Certificate of Excellence. Receiving the certificate was conditional on going to synagogue. At school, we wore a black uniform with a white collar and white buttons. When I was in third grade, my teacher gave me a storybook written in Polish calligraphy with four pictures of goats walking on a bridge. I sent my report to a competition in Warsaw, and I won a four-color gilt pen. From 1939 to 1941, I studied at a Russian school, which had students from the nearby villages.

Between 1939 and 1941, the Soviets conquered the area. They confiscated our property and built a sulfur factory on the land. The economic condition of the Jews deteriorated, but the Russians didn't resort to using violence. Warkowicze was once part of Poland in an area called Reichskommissariat (German occupation zones during WWII). During the war, Germany occupied many territories in Eastern Europe, and the borders between the countries changed.

The takeover of Warkowicze by the Russian army brought violence and crippled the economy. There was a shortage of provisions, and the townspeople stood in long lines to obtain food. Cigarettes were unavailable. My father could not give up smoking, so he'd make himself cigarettes from dried leaves from the cherry tree in our yard.

The Russian language took the place of Polish. That is how I learned to speak Russian, and I liked it. Under Russian rule, we lived relatively quietly. There were Jewish youths who joined Komsomol, the official communist youth movement in Russia.

On June 22, 1941, the Nazi Wehrmacht captured Warkowicze. They established a ghetto, surrounded by a barbed wire fence with a large gate. It was difficult to leave the ghetto, but the Jews managed to go out and barter with gentiles in the surrounding villages. Despite the enormous difficulties, the Jews celebrated all the Jewish holidays in secret. The Nazis appointed a Judenrat (a Jewish government institution that mediated between the Nazis and Jews). Shortly thereafter, they hanged three Jews who were Komsomol members. That was the first act of abuse against the Jews. Jewish survivors said that one of the Judenrat leaders committed suicide after being forced to hand over a Jewish woman to the German soldiers.

Every day, the Jews were taken into forced labor, run by Toot Corporation, a large German engineering company performing Nazi service. The Jews were transported to do road construction and fortification. The Germans humiliated the workers and beat them.

After six months, a few days after Passover of 1942, the Jews of Ozeryany arrived in Warkowicze. On October 8, 1942, four days after Simchat Torah, the Jews of both towns were loaded onto trucks and sent into the woods. A small number of Jews escaped, but they were later found and murdered by local policemen and peasants.

We lived in fear of the Nazi persecution. When rumor spread that the German army had occupied most of the area (about twenty-six kilometers north of Warkowicze), a cloud of concern descended upon us. We had not yet heard about what the Germans had done to Jews in other parts of Poland, so only a few Jews fled the town and went east. I was eleven at that time and was impressed by the proud appearance of the Germans in their uniforms, their big motorcycles, and military vehicles. What astonished me was the phrase that was embedded in their belt buckles: "God is with us."

One day, German soldiers came to our house and ordered us to stand outside. They entered our home and began to turn over the contents, looking for valuables. Anyone who tried to protest was beaten with their rifle butts.

All the Jews were ordered to wear a white ribbon with a Star of David, which later became a yellow badge on the left arm. Any Jew who was caught without a yellow badge risked his life. We were forbidden to leave our houses from dusk to dawn. During the day, young men and women were employed in forced labor inside and outside the town.

The first victims in our town were the three young Jews who had joined Komsomol. One of them was the daughter of Rabbi Gross. Her name was Chaika. Her sister Rochelle was a friend of mine. Many people attended the hanging.

Throughout the persecution, the Nazis had volunteer Ukrainian loyalists called Banderovches. They were antisemites who guarded and policed the ghetto. They wore black uniforms and were armed with rifles. In fact, we found them to be crueler than the Germans. At night, as we sat in our houses, we'd hear them outside singing their national anthem, which was forbidden during Russian rule.

It wasn't long before all the Jews were ordered to move into the ghetto at the end of town. The move was made on short notice, a few hours, so we could barely get organized. My father brought a trolley on which we loaded the most essential things, and we pulled it after us into the ghetto. Our family members numbered ten: grandmother Henia, my parents, myself, my brother Pinchas, my uncle Moses, his wife and his four-year-old daughter, my uncle Avraham, and his wife. We ten were assigned a small room without a toilet or kitchen. The night before moving into the ghetto, my father and Uncle Avraham dug a hole in the floor of the unfinished building and buried silverware and valuables, hoping that the next day they'd go back and retrieve them. Unfortunately, that day did not come.

The ghetto, as I said, was surrounded by a barbed wire fence with a large gate. Every day, young men and women went out in groups, under the Judenrat, to work on paving roads and other similar tasks. My father was made to work like a slave. Every morning, he went out to work with a group of Jews and came back in the afternoon. There were times when entire groups did not return from work, and we did not know their fate.

Initially, we ate the provisions that we had brought with us, but they soon ran out. The Judenrat tried to organize food distribution among the Jews of the ghetto, but it was not enough. Every family had to take care of themselves. Gentile peasants from the area would come to the ghetto fence with products to barter with the Jews. I do not remember being hungry in the ghetto. There was mutual help, and the Jews supported each other.

Once every few weeks, my mother would sneak out of the ghetto to obtain food for our family. She knew many of the peasants in the surrounding villages, and she spoke Polish, Ukrainian, and Czech. She would walk to one of the villages, sometimes trekking as far as ten kilometers away. I went with her to help carry the produce. Whenever we left the ghetto, we'd remove our yellow badges. With money in her hand, my mother bought bread, potatoes, onions, and other vegetables from the peasants. She put everything in a large sack and carried the heavy bag on her back. As I was only twelve years old, I carried the milk, butter, and cheese. When we got back and approached the ghetto, we had to put on our yellow badges again. The goods we bought were not allowed to enter the main entrance gate, so we placed them near the outside fence of our home and waited for one of the work groups to lead us into the ghetto. Generally, the relationship between ghetto Jews and the Judenrat and Jewish police officers was one of understanding and cooperation.

On October 8, 1942, four days after Simchat Torah, my mother and I went out on one of our trips to bring food into the ghetto. On our way back from one of the villages, about one kilometer from the ghetto, we heard a woman in the distance calling to us in Polish. As we approached her, she shouted that if we wanted to stay alive, we should leave the ghetto immediately because all the Jews were being led into the forest, and the Nazis were going to murder them. We turned back immediately and started walking quickly until we reached Peredil. We found shelter in the nearby forest and waited until we found out what happened in the ghetto that day. What we learned was that the Nazis and the Ukrainians surrounded the ghetto, set up trucks at the gate and ordered all the Jews to board them. Ferocious dogs stood by the trucks. We learned that the Jews were transported to the nearby forest. There, the Nazis ordered them to dig a large pit, take off their clothes and get into it. The Gestapo stood around the pit with their dogs and shot the Jews to death. The bodies were covered with lime. They killed all the residents of Warkowicze and Ozeryany. That included my family.

My mother and I were now left alone without a family. We had to think about our survival, especially with winter approaching. We were not dressed properly and had no money or valuables with which to buy warm clothes or winter shoes while suffering from cold and hunger. In the evenings, my mother would go to some of the peasants who had been kind to us to ask for food.

We looked for shelter in barns and slept in the hay. Often, the peasants would discover us and demand that we leave because our presence endangered their lives. At most, some were willing to give us food if we left immediately.

One morning, when we were hiding in the barn of a farmer named Bechowski, he went into the yard with his dog to see if there were any Jews hiding on his property. The dog discovered us. Luckily, the farmer allowed us to stay there until evening. From time to time, peasants like him would give us news about the war. On a few occasions, we hid in the yard of another farmer, who let us into his house to eat boiled potatoes with cream. Sometimes, the farmers would give us a few slices of bread.

Once, while hiding in a large haystack in a farmer's yard, we suddenly heard voices. My mother shook the straw, and we saw two girls—fifteen-year-old Sonia and her thirteen-year-old cousin Brunia. They told us that they had escaped from a horse-drawn wagon when Jews were being led into the forest to be executed. They spoke only Yiddish. We let them join us. We knew that this increased our risk, and friendly peasants even commented on it, but we couldn't leave them alone, especially since they could only speak Yiddish. The four of us stayed together throughout the war and were separated only for short periods. Most of the peasants in the surrounding villages were not antisemitic, but antisemitism remained our biggest fear.

Hiding in a haystack.

Miriam's Dream was not to leave the two girls she saved.

The Banderovches knew where the villages and farms were located, which enabled them to capture fugitive Jews. Through their sources, they knew that peasants were providing shelter for Jews. They made surprise searches in the villages to capture Jews and punish the peasants who hid them. We lived like persecuted animals. Wherever we were, we had to be cognizant of this danger. The peasants would warn us when a village raid was taking place, so we managed to escape elsewhere.

When the weather was favorable, we would stay outdoors, hiding in a narrow channel between two mountains near the Czech village of Martinovka and the Ukrainian village Novosilk, where Ukrainian peasants helped us. We would do hard work for the peasants in exchange for cooked food. In Novosilk, my mother was given a thick rope with which to knit snowshoe covers.

Once we gave one of the farmers in Martinovka a piece of clothing that Sonia had in exchange for twenty bowls of vegetable soup. The farmers invited us to eat at their home. Before we arrived, the farmer sent his daughters to check if there were Banderovche outside. As a precaution against the Banderovche attacking us while eating, his daughters guarded the outside of the house.

No longer exchanging my clothes for bread. Better days will come.

One time in the middle of winter, as we sat with this farmer eating soup, one of his daughters rushed unto the house and announced that a surprise search was underway in the village. We immediately ran outside to look for a way to escape. My mother started running toward the forest nearly half a mile from the village. A Banderovche saw her and started chasing her. Seeing that she was already far off, he started shooting at her. Then he took a horse and wagon from the farmer and chased her in the woods. She escaped from him, even though a bullet whizzed past her ear. I turned in another direction and ran barefoot through the snowy fields until the village houses disappeared. When I stopped and turned my head, I saw some distance on a path between Martinovka and Novosilk. I saw the Banderovche leading some captured Jews. Among the prisoners was a boy I knew, a neighbor from our village. He was held by two Ukrainians. The Jews were transported to a nearby forest and shot dead.

I hid in the grass for a few hours without moving until the Ukrainians were gone. When it was completely quiet, I got up and started walking. Sonia and Brunia had fled in different directions. I thought my mother had been caught and murdered, so I didn't try to look for them. I was twelve at the time and never cried. I headed toward Novosilk. As I walked down the street, people looked at me in amazement because I had wild, unruly hair and was dressed in ragged clothes that didn't fit the season. I left the village and wandered around to try to evaluate my surroundings.

In the evening, I met a Jewish woman named Rivka from Warkowicze. She told me that she was going to a village to find her children, whom she had left in a Polish mine. She asked me if I wanted to join her. I was reluctant to do so after hearing that the distance was very far. But Rivka didn't want to go alone at night, so she convinced me to join her. She assured me that we would find shelter near the mine. I agreed, and we walked all night. In front of us was a caravan of German jeeps. We were dazzled by the bright headlights. Somehow, we managed to evade them, and they didn't see us. The night was very dark and cold.

In the morning, we arrived at a secluded farm in Poland. The guard at the gate asked Rivka who I was. She answered in Yiddish that she didn't know, that I had come unexpectedly. That disturbed me greatly, after first not wanting to go with her and then agreeing to accompany her on that long trek. I had no idea where I was. Rivka went into the farmhouse, and I stayed outside. My legs froze and became swollen.

I hadn't eaten for a few days, so I was very hungry. I walked alone all night in the dark. Toward morning, I encountered some peasants and asked them for a piece of bread. They gave me a slice, and I kept going. On my way, one of the men chased away a little boy who wanted to hit me with a stick. I kept walking until I reached Peredil.

In Peredil, one of my aunt Raziel's neighbors, Gali, saw me in the village, which was filled with Banderovches. They followed me. I joined a group of shepherds tending their herds in the field, hoping that this would not attract attention. I stayed with them for a few hours. Then in the distance I saw two Ukrainians on bicycles, armed with weapons. When they approached, they started to question me: "What are you— Polish, Ukrainian or Jewish?" I recognized one of them. He was a young man who often frequented my aunt's shop and sometimes went to her house in the evenings with his friends to play cards. They brought me to the head of the Czech village of Solts. I slept in the loft on the wooden floor. A woman informed me that the locals intended to find and bring in more Jews and execute them in the woods. She urged me to run away. Later, the head of the village and his family were executed because they hid Jews in their home.

By a miracle, I saw my mother again and we found Sonia and Brunia as well.

In the spring of 1943, we hid for a while in a small grove near Novosilk. One day, a young Jewish couple who had fled the ghetto came to the grove. We lit a fire and spent time together drinking the coffee they had brought with them. We sat and sang songs to make ourselves feel less hungry. This is a Russian song that I remember:

> *There is darkness in the woods, and there is a bird that sings,*
> *And I am a boy in a strange land who has forgotten all his friends.*
> *No one will come, and no one knows,*
> *Only in the morning will the bird chirp.*

We stayed with the couple for a few nights. Then my mother decided that we should find another hiding place. At that time of year, casual work could be found in the peasants' yards. We decided to part company for a while and went to look for work. We told the peasants that the war had separated us from our families, and we were ready to do work for them in exchange for food and shelter.

My mother and Sonia went to a field of wheat and began to harvest with the laborers. I went to a nearby village and said that my parents were killed, and I was left alone and was ready to do whatever work was needed for a place to sleep and something to eat. A local family gave me work to do in the garden, in the barn and the chicken coop. After a few days, the landlady said I had a Jewish nose and that I'd better leave because she was afraid of being killed because of me.

The young couple we had met earlier decided to remain in the woods. We found them lying on the ground. Thinking that they were asleep, I went to wake up the man. Then I saw blood stains on his jacket. He was dead, and so was the woman. Apparently, they had been discovered by Ukrainian children who lured them to the Banderovches, who killed them.

The next day, after this heart-wrenching attack, we decided to leave Martinovka. We waited for the dark of night and crossed the frozen river and headed to Novosilk. We found an open pit and dried our wet clothes in it. A few days later, while hiding in a large haystack near the road, we heard a German vehicle stop near us. One of the Nazis came upon the haystack we were hiding in, and I heard him say, "Maybe there are dirty Jews here."

In Novosilk, we met Rabbi Gross from my town. He told us that he had seen my father and my brother on Yom Kippur. Just days later, he heard that they were killed in a mass murder in the forest. A few days after we met the rabbi, we heard from others that he had frozen to death in one of the buildings.

In the village, we met a devout Christian farmer who studied the Bible and had a large library in his home. He treated us very kindly. When Passover eve arrived, my mother asked him to make us a potato pie because we were not allowed to eat bread. He complied with her request. While the pie was cooking, we waited patiently at our usual spot near the village.

When we returned to him, he wanted to comfort us and show us what was written in the Scriptures about the Jews and what would happen to them. He read to us from a book that said there was going to be great trouble for the Jews, but they would be saved. The Jews would return to their country, and family members would find one another, even if they were a thousand miles apart.

At nights, we hid in villages in haystacks. On long, cold, dark nights when we couldn't find a place to sleep, we kept walking until we found shelter.

When the summer came, it was harvest season. My mother and Sonia looked for work in the fields in exchange for wheat or flour seeds. The peasants offered to help us with housework and in exchange they would grind wheat and bake bread for us.

One morning, my mother and Sonia went to the village of Fredil to ask the peasants to bake bread for them with the flour they had brought. Brunia and I waited for them on the channel near Novosilk. But by the afternoon they had still not returned, and we started to worry. They came back that evening in a panic, with no flour or bread. They said they had waited in the line to bake bread. As they waited, the son of this woman was a Banderovche and threatened to shoot them. The young man's mother and his fiancé begged him to leave them alone, but he refused. The two women held him tightly so that Sonia and my mother could escape. The Banderovche managed to get out of their grip and started chasing them. My mother and Sonia returned to us safely but with no food in their hands.

Another time, when my mother and Sonia were waiting in one of the farmers' houses for bread, German soldiers entered the house to take food. Luckily, there were several other people in the house who pretended to be members of the household, and that saved them.

When my mother went to one of the houses at night to ask for something to eat, a large dog got loose from its leash and attacked her. It bit her leg and tore off a piece of skin. The scar remained for life to remind her of the incident.

Under such harsh living conditions, we obviously could not maintain proper hygiene. Our hair was ridden with lice. Several kind Czech women helped us. They put our clothes in the oven to burn the lice. My hair was very long, and I tied it into two thick braids. One day, my mother decided to cut off all my hair. A Czech woman named Yagodova allowed me to shave my head in her kitchen. When I entered her hot kitchen, I fainted from the heat because I hadn't been in a heated house for years. The woman poured cold water on me to revive me.

It was 1943, and the four of us kept wandering around in search of food and shelter. One night while hiding in a haystack, we saw Elka Sapir from Warkowicze, who asked my mother for a piece of bread. Elka sang us a song in Yiddish, which I remember to this day.

After two years of struggling to survive under extremely difficult conditions, I began to despair. I told my mother that we should go to the Germans and give ourselves up. My mother said, "Absolutely not!"

In the winter of that year, many Russian soldiers were taken captive by the Germans. We hid in the barn of a Czech farmer. They employed a Russian soldier on the farm. It was very cold, so we asked the farmer to make us some hot vegetable soup. My mother received a full bowl of soup, which she started to carry to the barn. Suddenly she heard the Russian soldier whistling. In a panic, she began to run with the boiling-hot soup. It spilled on her, causing severe burns on her hands and blisters that became painful wounds. That night, we were left hungry and freezing.

In early 1944, when the German army began to withdraw from Russia, the four of us were once again hiding in a large haystack in the yard of a peasant near the road. A large column of cars passed by, watching German and Hungarian soldiers march down the road in retreat. The soldiers approached our haystack to take fodder for their horses and to look for fugitive Jews. They stabbed at the haystack with pitchforks but could not find us. Fearing that it might happen again, we left our hiding place in the dead of night and went down to the basement of the farmhouse.

Hiding from the Nazis.

The next morning, the landlady, who knew us, went down to the cellar to bring up some wine for the Russian soldiers. When she saw us, she told us that the Russian army had arrived and that we could leave the hideout without fear. At first, we suspected that she wanted to give us up. It was so hard for us to trust anyone. Finally, we decided to leave and went into her house and saw Russian soldiers. They spoke to us nicely, especially one of the officers. When we asked him his name, we found out that he was Jewish.

My mother and I realized that the war was over, at least for us in our area. I was 14 years old. We did not have even a photograph, any souvenir or proof of our existence. We had lost everything. The only survivors from our town were my mother, myself, my aunt Raziel and my cousin Rachel. All the rest (my father, brother, uncles, aunts, cousins, neighbors, friends, teachers, and townspeople) found their deaths in cruel and unimaginable ways, and we were never able to give them a proper burial.

At that point, we had no choice but to start from the beginning. We heard that in Rovno (Poland) there were homes for displaced Jews who had survived the war. The four of us decided to go there, where indeed we found many displaced refugees. It was then that we said goodbye to Sonia and Brunia and started our post-war life. For our livelihood, my mother would buy a large tray of pastries and sell them to the Turkish confectioner and the Russian soldiers who were walking around the city.

That was how we made a living until my mother became seriously sick with a blood-borne illness. I knew Dr. Tabacznik, who ran a hospital there. He said he could not help my mother and sent her to another hospital. During the time that my mother was ill, I sold thread, chocolates, pencils, cookies, rolls, and other items on the street. Since I did not have a vendor's license, I had to be very vigilant and flee whenever the inspectors came around. We cooked food for the partisans; in return, they gave us food. My mother and I moved from apartment to apartment several times. The city had been ransacked, and many apartments were deserted. We ended up living there. Most of the city was bombed every night, forcing us to go down to the basement for shelter and protection.

We lived in Rovno for about a year. We did not want to live under a communist regime, so we looked for a way to move to Poland. We met Lunie Vinokur, a mechanical engineer from Russia, who joined us. We used bribery to cross the border by train into Poland. Once we arrived, we went from place to place until we reached the city of Bytom. We heard that many Jews lived there because there was an organization (Hashomer Hatzair) that helped rescue displaced Jews. We rented a room with other members of the movement. To support my ailing mother, I worked selling rolls and beer to Russian soldiers. She was often in the hospital.

My cousin Rachel married a man name Shmilik in our apartment in Bytom. I gave them a blessing in Yiddish. From our apartment near Hashomer Hatzair, we moved to Sosnowiec. Until the outbreak of the war, Bytom had been the main center for preserving the national, social, and cultural Polish identity.

In 1945, after the liberation, we arrived in Germany at the Leipheim DP camp near Munich. We stayed there for about two years. My mother was ill and hospitalized in Munich. I visited her twice a week. I studied Hebrew in school. One night, I went to a Yiddish play called *Mirla–Efrat* and met emissaries from Israel. I asked them if they knew where Moshe Danai's family lived (Moshe was the brother of my aunt Raziel's husband).

They said they did and told me that the family owned an orange orchard. That is when I decided to move to Israel. Raziel had lost her husband and son in the war and later met a man named Hertz. She moved in with him in Ulm, Germany. During this time, my mother met a man named Nathan. They became a couple. As a result, we all went to Ulm and rented a room. We lived together: I, my mother, Rachel and Shmilik.

I belonged to a national youth movement called Gordonia for boys and girls who were new immigrants. In the evenings, we learned Hebrew, sang Hebrew songs, danced, and had a good time. I studied sewing as well.

I joined a group of young Jews whose goal was to immigrate to Israel and enlist in the army. I was the only girl in the group. Some of the guys wanted to travel to other places such as Canada and the US.

In October of 1948, I began my journey to immigrate to Israel. Our group of young Jews seeking to make aliya went through France, where we found a ship that was sailing to Israel. We were illegal immigrants. The timing was not the best—it was during the War of Independence.

I arrived alone and didn't know anyone in Israel. From the port, I went to a place called Agrobank, near Hadera. It was a temporary settlement for new immigrants, equipped with tents, cots and blankets. A man from the Culture Department of the government selected me to help fill out temporary immigration forms for new immigrants because I was fluent in Polish, Czech, Russian, Ukrainian, Hebrew, and Yiddish.

I decided not to enlist in the army because I was afraid that when my mother came to Israel she wouldn't be able to find me. When they asked me my age, I said I was born two years later, in 1932. I wanted them to think I was only sixteen.

My mother arrived in Israel two months later with her husband Nathan, whom she had married in Germany. After my short stay in Agrobank, I moved in with my mother and Nathan in Pardes Hanna, in their first home provided by the government. Nathan worked in the kitchen, which gave us the opportunity to have a constant supply of milk and jam.

My mother insisted that I learn a profession. I moved to Tel Aviv, where I lived with a woman named Zippora and her daughters Mira and Hadassah in the Yad Eliyahu neighborhood. I paid them 12 liras a month and helped with the household chores. I studied at the Secretariat Teacher Center to learn touch typing. Every morning, Zippora would make me an omelet sandwich to take to school. I found work sewing badges and emblems on IDF uniforms, which at that time was considered a good job.

Aunt Raziel moved to Kfar Saba, a city in the Sharon region in central Israel. By luck and mere chance, my mother and Nathan were given an apartment next door to Raziel in the Sirkin housing project of Kfar Saba. During the week I stayed in Tel Aviv; on the weekends, I went to Kfar Saba to be with my family.

When I lived in Tel Aviv, I was nineteen years old and single. Friends tried to fix me up with suitable guys. Finally, I met Joseph. I liked him very much and wanted to get married. During this period, Israel restricted the purchase of food and consumer goods. Every citizen who went to a grocery store received basic goods for points allocated to him/her in a personal ledger. We bought small measured quantities of sugar, flour oil, salt, and more. Aunt Raziel raised chickens. Chickens were considered a luxury item in Israel and were not sold in the markets. This created an opportunity for Raziel to sell chickens on the black market at higher prices.

He purchased eggs and, on occasion, a chicken from my aunt Raziel. My aunt thought that Joseph was a perfect match for me. He was a little older than me, born in 1925. He was also from Poland and a Holocaust survivor, having passed through five camps during the war. At age twenty-three, Joseph had made aliya, on May 15, 1948—the date that Israel became a state. When he arrived in Israel, he was handed a gun and was told that he had to fight in the war. He was sent to Latrun. When he got there, he developed a fever and was sent to the hospital—that is what saved him. All his friends died in that war.

The first time I met Joseph, he showed up at my aunt Raziel's house riding a bicycle. He was handsome, funny and smart, with a sound talent in commerce. His cousin Zosha, who had also survived the Holocaust, lived in Kfar Saba. She owned properties and a factory, producing skincare products, in that city. That is why Joseph chose to live there. He had a small apartment in the Mizrachi Second Housing with a bathroom and kitchen, which were shared with the neighbors.

After three months of dating, Joseph and I got married. The wedding was held in Zosha's house on May 30, 1950.

Joseph and I continued to live in Kfar Saba. As our family grew, we moved about five times, purchasing larger and larger apartments to accommodate us. We have three children: Fruma (1951) lives in Kfar Saba, Zvika (1956) lives in Pardes Hanna, and Oshrat (1967) lives in Ra'anana.

Miriam and her husband Joseph on their first date in Tel Aviv, 1949.

Wedding of Miriam Greenshepoon and her husband Joseph.

Joseph was a hard worker and held many different jobs in order to support the family. He first started to work at the post office. At night, he worked as a guard at his aunt's leather factory. Then he worked at the government employment office. He also worked in construction as a project manager for Meir Hospital. The owner of the Sharon Center events hall offered him a partnership position. Ultimately, Joseph worked for thirty-seven years as the manager of a school for mentally challenged children in Kfar Saba. He always brought kids to our home for Shabbat and Passover. He then did the same work at a facility in Herzliya for mentally challenged adults. Everyone liked my husband. Through all his years of hard work, he saved money which enabled him to purchase apartments for our children. Joseph died in 1986 at the age of 62.

I have fifteen grandchildren, seven of whom are married. I have eighteen great-grandchildren, with two more on the way. Zvika and Fruma each have four children, and Oshrat has seven. All my grandchildren held combat positions in the IDF such as Golani and Givati. They are all devout Orthodox Jews. Fruma is an interior designer, who also designs Jewish marriage certificates (*ketubot*), which she sells worldwide. Oshrat is also an artist. Zvika works in the goose liver trade in Europe. I think Zvika has the spirit of my late husband, and that to me is wonderful. Our family is very close, and that means everything to me.

Miriam with four out of her fifteen grandchildren.

Miriam with her family.

I started drawing at the age of eighty. My drawings depicted the harsh memories I experienced during the Holocaust. The illustrations were simple caricatures of people that expressed my deepest, darkest secrets. Drawing was a way to release repressed memories that haunted my childhood. In all, I drew about fifteen or twenty illustrations. The drawings had no conventional path or plan but were spontaneous. I used a pen or pencil and drew on whatever material was handy such as postcards, envelopes and scratch paper.

After I moved from my apartment in Kfar Saba to a retirement home, my apartment remained vacant with all my personal belongings. After two years of my living in the home for the elderly, Fruma and Oshrat cleared out my apartment so it could be rented. They spent countless arduous hours going through all the items that I had amassed over my lifetime. Sifting through each item, they were able to recover my drawings. On the enclosed balcony there were cardboard boxes filled with items that withered due to the dampness of wet winters: this is where my daughters found most of my best works.

Chapter Three

Building on a Dream

Mordechai Mark

My name is Mordechai Mark. I was born on November 6, 1927, in the town of Iara de Mureş in northern Transylvania. My first name while living in Europe was Elemer. It was changed to Mordechai when I immigrated to Israel in 1961.

My mother, Helen, was born in 1905. In Hungarian, her name was Elomoka Taisman. She was born and raised in the village of Târnăveni, some sixty kilometers from our village. My mother had one sister and two brothers, all of whom perished during the Holocaust. During World War II, Târnăveni was decimated, including the synagogue.

My father, Isadore, was born in 1897. He was the youngest of five brothers. His four brothers perished during the Holocaust. My father was born and raised in the village of Iara de Mureş. He married my mother when he was 30 years old. My parents were married through the introduction of a matchmaker. In those days, a matchmaker was a professional who was paid a fee. Transylvania used the dowry system for newlyweds. The usual marital custom required the bride's family to give the groom and/or his family cash, jewelry, electrical appliances, furniture, bedding, crockery, utensils, property or other household items to help the newlyweds set up their home. My parents' wedding took place in a private home with a small gathering of family and friends. The ceremony was officiated by a rabbi.

My grandparents were married under very unusual circumstances. My grandfather attended a wedding, but the groom did not show up, so the rabbi selected my grandfather to step up in his place to be the groom. That is how he married my grandmother. They were happily married until their deaths in WWII.

I had one brother, Alexander, who later changed his name to Shlomo. He was two years older than me. In those days, we did not have hospitals. I was delivered by a midwife in a private home in Iara de Mureş (part of the municipality of Comuna Gornesti and Judetul Mureş province in the central part of Romania, 270 kilometers north of Bucharest). We were one of two Jewish families living in the village, which had a population of not more than twenty. At home we spoke Hungarian and Romanian, but I could speak Yiddish as well.

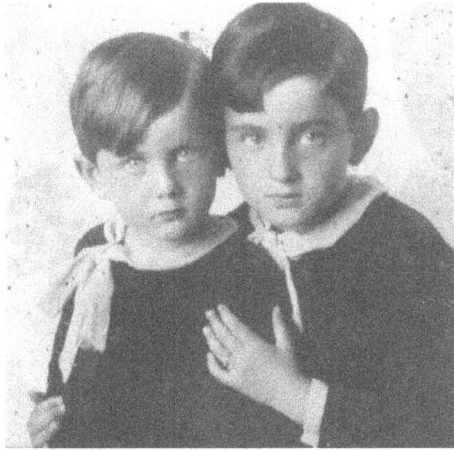

Mordechai, three-years-old, with his seven-year-old brother Shlomo.

Mordechai's parents with his younger sister.

We lived in Iara de Mureş for one year, then moved to the agricultural village of Sărăţeni, which had a population of about 500 people, twenty of whom were Jews. Sărățeni became an independent commune after, in 2004, it split from the town of Sovata, some five kilometers from Iara de Mureș. We lived there until the advent of WWII.

My grandfather owned large tracts of land used for agriculture, which were handed down to my father. My father was a passionate farmer who also owned and operated a store on the property. That was our main source of income. We had horses, cows, chickens, and other livestock. We made our own butter with a handmade machine and had fresh milk daily from our cows. During my holidays from school and on the weekends when I was home, I worked on the farm and in the store. Nearby, there was one other store owned by a gentile. The only transportation was by horse and buggy. It was only four or five months before the war that I had a bicycle. We had good relationships with the gentiles. When the events of WWII began, our relationship with the gentiles soured.

Sovata was a popular health resort at the end of the nineteenth and twentieth century because of its salty lakes and warm water. There was a synagogue, a Jewish school, and a kosher butcher. The demographic makeup was Hungarian and Romanian. I went to school in Sovata from kindergarten until fourth grade (1938). Although it was only five kilometers away from our home, my father preferred that I live in Sovata, so he arranged for me to rent a room in a home owned by a Jewish family he knew. Most of the Jews in Sovata were traditional. They observed Shabbat and kept kosher. Rarely did I see Hassidic Jews there.

Family home in Sărățeni, Tranvsylvania.

Family home in Târnăveni, Transylvania.

When I was eleven, I moved to Târgu Mureş, some fifty kilometers from my home. I studied there from fifth grade until high school at a technical school. Because of the war, I was unable to complete my high school education. My father rented a room for me in the home of a Jewish family, so I had a place to sleep close to my school. I went to my family home as often as possible on the weekends and during vacations. It was when I was in middle school that I started to hear words of antisemitism.

When I was growing up in Transylvania, parents taught their children to respect their elders. This was a significant element in the community. It is worth noting that my parents never argued nor did my friends and neighbors. The atmosphere was serene and calm.

Morderchai's father, Isadore after losing his eyesight from an explosion at the factory where he worked.

By the summer of 1941, some 18,000 Jews were evicted from their homes and deported to Kamenets-Podolsk in Ukraine, where most of them were murdered. In early 1942, another 1,000 Jews in the part of Yugoslavia newly acquired by Hungary were murdered by Hungarian soldiers and police in their pursuit of partisans.

From 1937 to 1944, the government in Transylvania was under Hungarian rule. The party in power from October 15, 1944, until March 28, 1945, was the Nyilaskeresztes Párt, or Arrow Cross Party, otherwise known as the Government of National Unity, led by Frederic Szálasi. During its rule, 10,000 to 15,000 civilians (many of whom were Jews and Romanians) were murdered, and 80,000 people were deported from Hungary to various concentration camps in Austria. The party was inspired by the Nazis: in fact, their Arrow Cross emblem was taken from an ancient Hungarian tribe that believed in racial purity of the Hungarians just as did the Nazis of the Aryan race. After the war, Szálasi and other Arrow Cross leaders were tried as war criminals by Hungarian courts.

On March 19, 1944, Hungarian soldiers started to enter our town. Up until that date, we had not been subjected to the atrocities, annihilation, and murder of Jews across Europe by the Nazis. We didn't have any radios or phones, so we fashioned a radio from a battery and percolator. Still, we didn't know what was happening around us.

On May 3, 1944, at 7 a.m., the Hungarian Royal Gendarmerie rounded up the Jews from all the villages in the Mureș region, totaling some 8,000—all within twenty-four hours. We didn't know why or where we were going. If we had known that they were planning to kill us, everyone would have run away.

The soldiers told us, "You have one hour to take your things." They said we couldn't take more than seventy kilos, two suitcases, and not to worry about our properties. My father was forty-seven years old. He took one suitcase by hand, and the other one he carried on his back. We put everything on a wagon and began to walk behind the carts. Our family numbered ten people. When the non-Jews witnessed the roundup, they gave us food.

We walked four kilometers to Sovata. Then from Târgu Mureș, we took a truck. We were taken to an abandoned factory that made construction blocks, which had a lake nearby. When we arrived, the Hungarian soldiers began stealing jewelry from us. They even got some people to confess where they lived, and later robbed their houses. People who had jewelry and other items of value threw them into the lake so the soldiers wouldn't find them.

As we were ascending the ramp to the train that was destined for Auschwitz, the soldiers told my father that he could not take the suitcases aboard the train. That was a big turning point in my life—to see the pain and suffering that my father had gone through, having carried two suitcases four kilometers, and then not being allowed to take our belongings with us. All of us (more than seventy people) entered the train car (used for transporting goods and livestock), where we stood packed in like sardines. The car had two windows and two buckets. One bucket was for water, and the other was a urinal. We covered the urinal bucket with a coat. We traveled for three days on the train, thinking that we were going to work in a better place. Having my family nearby gave me strength and hope. I remember seeing my uncle, who lived in Sovata and was a devout Orthodox Jew, praying against the wall with two pairs of tefillin.

When we arrived at the border, I heard the conductor use the hammer to hit the steel wheels. That gave me hope that the train was going to continue. The train finally stopped in Auschwitz, Poland. It was about 5 a.m. on Monday, the first day of Shavuot. The guards opened the doors of all the rail cars and began ordering everyone to get off the train.

When we arrived at Auschwitz, the Sonderkommandos, who had already been working there for three years, told us to leave all our belongings on the train. Sonderkommandos were special units made up of German Nazi death camp prisoners. They were composed of prisoners, usually Jews, who were forced, on threat of their own deaths, to assist the Nazis in killing Jews in the gas chambers. The death camp Sonderkommandos, who were always inmates, were unrelated to the SS Sonderkommandos, which were *ad hoc* units formed from various SS officers between 1938 and 1945.

When I saw the fire and smokestack, I asked the Sonderkommando what this was. He said those pass a certain line end up in smoke. I was in shock that I was facing my potential death. I never heard any noises, I only know through others telling me that Jews were being killed in gas chambers.

There were two lines—left and right. That was when I saw Josef Mengele (known as the Angel of Death for his lethal genetic experiments on prisoners) using his finger to point the Jews to go either to the right or to the left. Those on the right went to the labor camp; those on the left went straight to the crematorium. People who were over forty or fifty years of age went to the crematorium. Because my aunt and grandmother were elderly, the Nazis ordered them to stand in line for the crematorium, and that was the last I saw of them. My mother didn't want to be separated from her mother, so she joined her. Out of love and compassion for my grandmother who was 65 years old, my mother, 39-years-old, gave up her life, joined her in the line for the crematorium, to die together.

My grandfather had died long before in Iara de Mureş. Even at this point, we didn't know for sure what was going on.

My brother, uncle, father, cousin, and I were told to go to the right to work in the labor camp. The Sonderkommandos told us to remember our clothes and our numbers. After the prisoners died in the showers, the Sonderkommandos removed their gold teeth, eyeglasses and other things of value. Luckily, my family remained intact. We received our identity numbers, which were stitched on our striped work clothes. The numbers were not inscribed on our forearms like a tattoo as was common for most Jews. The guards took all our personal belongings. They shaved all the hair on our heads except for a strip down the middle of the head to identify us as prisoners. It was a security measure to deter us from escaping. We could keep only our shoes and belts.

The Sonderkommandos took us to our barracks, which included all the Jews that were on our train. Our family stayed together in one barrack— my father and brother, my two uncles, cousin, and I. The barracks had double and triple wooden bunk beds. After two days, the Germans gave us a postcard on which to write to our relatives. Later, we discovered that they threw the postcards away. In the coming days, we were sent in different groups to work in the forest.

We were asked about our work experience and professions. Being sixteen and a half years old, I was strong both mentally and physically, and the guards knew this. The guards were called kapos. A kapo prisoner functionary was a prisoner in a Nazi concentration camp who was assigned by the SS guards to supervise forced labor or carry out administrative tasks. If they were derelict in their job, they would be returned to the status of ordinary prisoners and be subjected to other kapos. Many prisoner functionaries were recruited from the ranks of violent criminal gangs rather than from the more numerous political, religious, and racial prisoners. Such criminal convicts were known for their brutality toward other prisoners. This brutality was tolerated by the SS and was an integral part of the camp system.

We were malnourished and incredibly weak, facing imminent death. Our lack of food coupled with hard labor led to many deaths including that of my uncle.

Between the barracks there was an electric fence. Those who lost hope and were in utter despair threw themselves onto the electric fence and died instantly. Every day after work, we were exhausted, malnourished, and barely hanging on. The kapos took the weak out of the barracks and beat them to death to reduce the population of Jews. They had personal goals to kill a certain quota of Jews in order to meet the demands of the Nazis and the overcrowded conditions. We wrote our names on a piece of wood with the hope that other prisoners from neighboring barracks would let others know we were alive.

After two days in Auschwitz, we were put on another train. We underwent a grueling seven-day journey, traveling 554 kilometers to the Mauthausen concentration camp in Austria. Again, there were 70 of us standing on our feet, with almost no sleep. Even with everything that I had witnessed, we were like stones, little lambs being herded to the slaughter.

After traveling almost 300 kilometers, we arrived in Vienna. The guards opened the doors to give us some air and to change the urinal and water buckets. I saw how elegantly dressed the Viennese people were and just didn't understand why this was happening to us. It was apparent to me from the Austrians who opened the train doors that there was a thick stench of antisemitism.

We continued our journey for another 165 kilometers to Mauthausen. When we got off the train, the first thing we saw was a sign in German that read "Arbeit macht frei" (Work sets you free).

There were three Gusen contraction camps (Gusen 1-3) in and around the village of St. Georgen/Gusen, just five kilometers from Mauthausen. Gusen 1 was the first. The newest one was Gusen 2.

The inmates of Mauthausen and its subcamps were forced to work as slave labor, under conditions that caused many deaths. Mauthausen and its subcamps included quarries, munitions factories, mines, arms factories and plants that assembled fighter aircrafts. In January 1945, the camps contained roughly 85,000 inmates. The death toll remains unknown. Out of approximately 320,000 prisoners throughout the war, approximately 80,000 survived.

Mauthausen had the largest labor camp complexes in the German-controlled part of Europe and was the last to be liberated by the Allies.

These were the toughest camps, mostly used for extermination through labor of the educated people and members of the higher social classes. Many large German companies used laborers from Mauthausen. Prisoners were rented out to work on local farms, road construction, reinforcing and repairing the banks of the Danube, and the construction of large residential areas. They were also forced to excavate archeological sites. Mauthausen was one of the few camps to use a mobilized improvised gas chamber on a regular basis.

Other groups of people to be persecuted solely on religious grounds were Bible students, or as they are called today, Jehovah's Witnesses, as well as many Poles (non-Jews) including artists, scientists, Boy Scouts, teachers, and university professors.

In Mauthausen, prisoners worked in the quarries in unbearable temperatures, as low as −30 °C (−22 °F), which led to exceptionally high mortality rates. The food rations were so limited that an average inmate weighed 40 kilograms. Food rations dropped from about 1,750 calories a day to 1,460 to 1,150. By 1945, the rations dropped from 1,000 to 600 calories per day, which led to the starvation of thousands of inmates.

Prisoners were forced to carry blocks of stone often weighing as much as 50 kilos up 186 stairs, one prisoner behind the other. They called this the "Stairs of Death." Many of the prisoners collapsed in front of the other prisoners in the line, and then fell on top of the others, creating a domino effect all the way down the stairs. The SS guards would often force prisoners to race up the stairs carrying the stone blocks. Those who survived the ordeal would often be placed in a line-up at the edge of a cliff known as "The Parachutists Wall." At gunpoint, each prisoner would have the option of being shot or pushing the prisoner in front of him off the cliff.

Other means they used to kill prisoners included death in bunkers, hangings, and mass shootings. At times, the guards would throw the prisoners onto the 380-volt electric barbed wire fence or force them outside the boundaries of the camp and then shoot them on the pretext that they were attempting to escape. Some 3,000 inmates died of hypothermia, having been forced to take an icy cold shower and then be left outside in the cold weather. Many inmates were drowned in barrels of water.

Within two or three weeks, our family was separated. The guards created groups to allocate us according to our previous working skills. There were 200 to 300 people in each group, in groups of five in each line. I was in the first line. My brother was transferred to the Ebensee concentration camp in Austria. Its main focus was to build tunnels for armaments storage. My father and cousin were transferred to other work camps as well.

From Mauthausen, I walked five kilometers in the rain to Gusen 1. It was the oldest and had everything, with a crematorium including showers. However, Gusen 2 was new, so there was nothing but stones and barracks. It was one of the worst work camps. Two days after my arrival in Gusen 2, I was assigned to work in the Knalbo—a water treatment plant. The prisoners had belts and shoes made from trees. My father had given me shoes. I exchanged them for food with the guards. I was starving and had no other choice—my calorie intake was far below the needs of a functioning human being. The guards wanted my shoes, so in exchange they gave me food, as the amount of calorie intake was far below the needs of any functioning human being.

The kapos were assigned to kill at least twenty prisoners per day. The victims were those who were weak and totally fatigued. The Nazis took the weak and beat them to death with a stick. The guards took the dead bodies by horse trailer to the crematorium in Gusen 1.

The SS officer who was German/Hungarian saw that I was strong both mentally and physically. For that reason, he gave me a better job than the others. My job in Gusen was to remove the plates after the prisoners were fed. I arrived in Gusen 2 on June 18, 1944, and stayed until April 1945, doing the same work. It was an ideal job because I was able to take leftover food from the kitchen, so I was never malnourished.

One of the most emotional moments of my stay in Gusen was when other prisoners approached me and offered me their gold teeth in exchange for food. It was heart-wrenching. Of course, I never accepted anything from my fellow prisoners.

One day, I went to visit a friend in the hospital at the camp and saw a doctor who was from Sovata. He recognized me and asked me if I remembered him. I did not, but it turns out that he had been in love with my mother and they had intended to get married. He said, "Do you know that I was supposed to be your father?"

I worked in airplane factories underneath bunkers, working day and night. One day, standing between two industrial buildings, I fell asleep on the road. An SS officer asked me what I was doing. I was so scared, that I wet my pants. I was afraid that he was going to kill me. Fortunately, the officer walked away and left me alone.

By March 1945, I saw that the Germans were retreating. Suddenly, we didn't work for two days because there was a revolt within Hitler's regime to remove him and replace him with new leadership. They didn't succeed, and all the rebels were killed.

I remember climbing to the top of a mound of dirt collected between the two barracks. I saw the Germans retreating, and the Americans marching toward our camp. I was so excited that I jumped up and hit the electric wire. Luckily, the 220 volts flung me away from the wire and saved me from being electrocuted. Others from my camp came to my rescue and took me to the camp for the "appel." It was the periodic head count the Germans took to keep track of the prisoners to ensure that nobody escaped or had died. When I was standing in the line, one of the prisoners told me to put my hand in the dirt to eliminate the static electricity.

Two days later, the Germans gave an order to gather all the Jews and transport them to the crematorium. There were prisoners from all over Europe, but the order was for the Jews only to be sent back to Mauthausen. They organized us in groups of five. The Germans saw the end of the war and were in a hurry to kill the remaining Jews, otherwise known as the "Final Solution."

When I arrived in Mauthausen, I was placed in an open field with other people. Then I heard a voice say, "Does anyone know Elmer Mark?" The man speaking was my father. He was very thin but functioning. I had taken a piece of meat from the kitchen from Gusen, and I gave it to him. At that point, I saw other arrivals wearing nice clothes who were staying in tents until being transported to work camps. This was their first stop. Instead of eating the meat, my father found his cousin and traded the meat for clothes without stripes and a coat so I could have a good night's sleep. The Germans gathered us in an area, enclosed by a metal fence.

In groups of five, we walked more than fifty kilometers from Mauthausen to the Gunskirchen labor camp. That trek took three days. Along the way, we found potatoes in the fields. Luckily, we had brought a pot in which to cook them over a fire. We slept in the open fields. An SS officer asked my father if he had stolen the potatoes, but he said that others had given them to him. The officer would have killed my father if he had admitted to stealing the potatoes.

My father was forty-eight years old, and I was seventeen. Two days after leaving the fields, we arrived at Gunskirchen. When we got there, an

SS officer told me that the Germans had lost the war and were leaving. It was Friday night, May 5, 1945, when we were liberated.

Within one or two weeks after we were liberated, thousands of Jews died. Their bodies were skin and bones, too weak to function. When we were released, nobody was happy. We were like stones from everything that we had experienced. By May 6, 1945, the war was declared over.

After being released from Gunskirchen, we came upon a sugar and coffee storage building. The other prisoners, who were famished, ran to the building and devoured the sugar. I took a sack and filled it with coffee and sugar and knew not to eat it. Most of us were so thin and malnourished that the consumption of too much sugar in our system would make our bodies collapse. That caused many of my fellow prisoners to die. My cousin was one of those victims.

We walked in the direction of Wels, Austria, which was twelve kilometers away. On the way, we stopped at a large abandoned house and slept outside in the chicken coop. We killed a chicken and cooked it over a fire. I was with my father and a cousin. A few of the prisoners stayed in the house.

Two days later, we arrived in Wels. The Americans who were occupying the German army base in Wels found us. They gave us food, rooms, clothes, and medical treatment. It was like being in a five-star hotel. We were so hungry that we ate the leftovers on the plates. After we settled in, the Americans sprayed us with DDT to remove infections and diseases. The soldiers asked us where we wanted to go. They were ready to give us cash and a new life wherever we wanted, including the US. I remained in the camp for a few months. Others who had been released from other camps came to our camp as well.

We were trying to find friends and family. I heard that my brother was alive. My uncle and aunt had died after being released from Gunskirchen.

We had to be careful because the Russians were taking Jews to Siberia. One of my friends was taken to Siberia for three years.

My father and I told the Americans that we wanted to go back home to Transylvania. We passed through Czechoslovakia along the Danube River. In Slovakia, we started to see Russian soldiers in Bratislava on trucks and horses with trailers. The Russians told us we couldn't take anything—this was communist Eastern Europe. They took us to nearest train station to return to our home in Târgu Mureș.

My father had tefillin and a tallit. A Russian soldier stole it from him, thinking it was something of monetary value. My father ran after him and retrieved it, risking his life. He could have been sent to Siberia.

We took a transport train, where we sat on the top of the caboose. It was very dangerous, as we could have fallen off. We traveled through Budapest to Oradea in Romania, which had previously been part of Hungary. On August 23, 1945, the Russians gave Transylvania back to Romania.

When we arrived in Oradea, we were taken to a hospital for Jews. Before we went to sleep, Dr. Miklós Nyiszl came to see us. He was a Jewish Sonderkommando who had worked for Mengele and lived in Oradea. For half the night, he talked about what he had seen in Auschwitz and Birkenau. We never knew anything. In 1946, he wrote a book about the experiments he performed. He had been Mengele's right-hand man.

After spending two days in Oradea, we took the train 200 kilometers to Târgu Mureș. We stayed for one night and went to a Jewish hospital. Then we took a bus to our house, which was 40 kilometers from Sovata. We heard that my brother had been living in the house for two months. When we arrived, it was sad to be home without our family. The Russians had taken all our possessions.

In 1945, the communists were in power, and "democracy" and "capitalism" were words of the past. The government owned everything.

Initially, my father and brother returned to work on our farm and in the store. However, we soon learned that this was a futile attempt to make a living because the communists owned everything. Working on the farm and in the store didn't make economic sense, so the only way to earn a living was to work in a state-owned factory.

My aunt and uncle had owned and operated a gas station about twenty kilometers away. They had been killed in the war, so the business was abandoned, and their cars and gas tanks were stolen. My brother decided to take over the business and began importing gas from Bucharest.

I was only seventeen years old. Because of the war, I was unable to finish high school. I returned to the technical school in Târgu Mureș. After two years, I obtained my high school diploma.

Once we realized that living in Romania was a dead end, we began to hear that Jews were immigrating to Israel. I became a member of a Zionist organization, and for the next year and a half I started to learn more about agriculture so I could immigrate in Israel and live on a kibbutz. By 1948, the Romanian government closed the Zionist organization, thus forcing us to work in government-owned factories. This led many Jews to move to Israel.

I left Sovata in 1945 and moved to Târnăveni (Turnevin). I worked in a factory for several years, then went to work in a chemical factory in a managerial position.

My brother made aliya in 1948. With the money he earned importing gas, he paid a man in Varna, Bulgaria, to get him a permit to travel to Israel, which never came to fruition. Eventually, however, he obtained his travel permit and took the last ship from Varna to Haifa, Israel.

Mordechai and his father, 1948.

My father made aliya in 1950. From the Romanian city of Constanza near the Black Sea, he took a ship to Haifa. He was fifty years old. Around that time, the Romanian government stopped issuing permits to Israel. One of my cousins went directly to Israel after being released from a concentration camp.

I met Yehudit Mandel in Târnăveni. She was a bookkeeper in the factory where I worked. We were married in 1952. Our wedding took place in the garden of a private home in Reghin (twenty-nine kilometers northeast of Târgu Mureș), a community that had about 6,000 Jews before the war. Our wedding was a small and intimate affair, officiated by a rabbi. My cousin and my wife's sister arranged the event. One memorable moment was taking pictures of our wedding. In communist Romania, which was just an extension of communist Russia, there was no modern equipment—everything was antiquated. Our photographer had worked in Africa as a cameraman. His equipment was obsolete compared to Western civilization, but functional. He placed a black drape over his head to take a still photograph. He had only one slide (film). Fortunately, the picture turned out well. It was the only picture of our wedding.

Mordechai with friends in Romania, 1953.

Mordechai and Yehudit's wedding.

Mordechai and Yehudit, 1950.

After getting married, I applied for a travel permit to Israel. Through self-determination, after ten years (1961), I finally obtained my travel permit, overcoming endless red tape imposed by communist bureaucrats. The Romanian government required me to certify that our apartment was clean and ready for the next person to move in. In the interim, our son Zeev was born, in 1955.

Yehudit, her friends, and family at her parents' house in Târnăveni.

My wife, Zeev and I took a train from Târnăveni to Vienna, where we were met by the Jewish Agency. In Vienna, I telephoned my father to let him know that we were coming to Israel. During the time away from my father and brother, we communicated by letters. A few days later, we took a train to Naples, Italy, and then took a ship to Haifa. Zeev was five years old. It was Yom Kippur, and I remember a religious Jew taking away my son's bread.

Yehudit and her sisters.

We could not take money with us, only jewelry and other small personal items that could fit into a pocket. The Jewish Agency allowed each person a maximum of seventy kilos of luggage. The Agency gave us some money.

My brother Shlomo had arrived in Haifa before Israel was a state. It was then under British-controlled Palestine (1918-1948). The British did not allow my brother to disembark in Haifa and forced his ship to sail to Cyprus. For the next year and a half, Shlomo lived in a Cyprus internment camp, along with some 52,000 Jews from all parts of Europe. They had been taken off thirty-nine ships in their attempt to get to Palestine. During all that time, I did not know where my brother was.

Shlomo left Cyprus and sailed to Israel. Once he arrived in Israel, he chose to start his life in Petach Tikva and established a business transporting construction material. My father lived in Tel Aviv and worked as a messenger at a private bank.

My in-laws lived in Bat Yam in a government housing for new immigrants. Prior to making aliya, my father-in-law worked in the US in a factory that made explosive materials. There was an accident and he became blind. He was compensated with a lifetime pension from the company, paid in US dollars. This allowed his family to live a comfortable life in Romania and Israel.

When our ship docked in Haifa, the Jewish Agency directed us to live in an immigration housing compound in Netanya. Zeev laughed with delight when he saw how much sand there was in Israel for him to play. When we arrived in Netanya, I went to the post office to call my father, and out of nowhere I saw my brother.

We left Netanya with Shlomo in his car. We went to live with my in-laws, who resided in a two-story housing absorption center in Bat Yam. Our first objective was to learn Hebrew. For the next six months, we took three buses to get to Petach Tikva to learn Hebrew at an ulpan for eight hours a day. We only knew Hungarian, Romanian, and Yiddish. We didn't have much money. I remember paying one shekel to buy two eggs and a piece of bread at the corner store. Other new immigrants in my class were from South Africa, and were financially well off.

Ulpan in Israel, 1964.

Mordechai and his brother Shlomo upon their arrival to Israel.

We left Bat Yam and moved to an apartment in Givat Shmuel, which was given to us by the Jewish Agency. We lived there for a year. Then in 1964, we moved to Petach Tikva, where we purchased our first apartment from the Rasco Construction Company. During that period, Israel was in a recession. We benefited from the situation and received a 20% discount on the price of the apartment. Not only that, but the contractor agreed to allow us to pay in installments. Our apartment was on the seventh floor of a twelve-story luxury high-rise apartment building with an elevator.

In 1967, I began working with Shlomo's construction company in Petach Tikva, called Shimshon, which transported construction materials. This was my first foray into working as an independent person. Yehudit worked as our bookkeeper. My central role was to coordinate the logistics of moving the construction materials from each job site. Our office was in the same building as our apartment. We didn't have a phone in the office, so we had to pull telephone wire from our apartment, through the window, to the office.

After the Six-Day War of 1967, we signed a purchase and sale agreement to buy a piece of undeveloped agriculture land. The owner agreed to extend the payments over a long period of time. Since we were a young company, we lacked capital resources. Thinking out of the box, I contacted Azorim, one of Israel's largest and oldest real estate development and construction companies, and managed to sell our purchase contract rights to them. We sold the land for a profit and became the general contractors that built their project of sixty-four apartments.

In 1967, I formed a company called A. Mark and made my brother a partner. Shlomo became ill, so I was faced with the challenge of managing the company on my own. I continued to focus our activities on transporting construction materials and found new business opportunities in Beersheba and Dimona. In Dimona, we found a project to build an asphalt factory. I developed close relationships with Israel's largest contractors. I believed in taking small steps rather than shooting for the stars for quick short-term growth. Many other construction companies that took on huge projects and created massive debt soon failed and went bankrupt.

From the income I earned under A. Mark, I created a tax scheme, approved by the Supreme Court of Israel, which allowed me to offset the income earned under my company with the losses from the Shimshon Company. Over a period of four years, all the debts accumulated under Shimshon were paid in full, and the company was formally closed.

In 1978, I formed a company called Bonei Binyan Upituach Ltd. with Eliezer Meidanek, whom I knew from before as head of construction for the Ramet Company. We were equal partners. Ramet was one of the top-ranked construction firms in Israel. Eliezer was born and raised in Romania and had made aliya before me. Our activities were focused on the construction and transportation of construction materials. Shlomo was a partner, even though he was incapacitated due to health issues. I ran the finance and commercial side of the business, while Eliezer handled construction. Our priorities were focused solely on participating in third-party tenders through the State of Israel for construction projects in public works.

Over a period of ten years, we continued to participate in government tenders. Construction companies were ranked on a scale of one to five, five meaning the biggest and the ones with the strongest balance sheet. We, of course, started at the number one level, taking on projects relative to that size. As time went by, we won more tenders and gradually took on larger projects, ultimately reaching level five. Our company remained a solid, stable construction firm. To date, we have built around 400 projects throughout Israel in public works (such as schools, municipal buildings, hospitals). My brother Shlomo died in 1981.

In 1995, we moved from our office in Petach Tikva to Ra'anana, where we purchased an office unit on Levi Eshkol Street. Zeev graduated from the Technion in Haifa in civil engineering and started to work for me in 1983.

My partner Eliezer died in 2008. We had a successful partnership for thirty years, never having a significant disagreement. In 2014, we sold our ownership interest to Eliezer's son, Haim Median (Meidanik), and started a new construction company. I worked with Zeev until I was 88 years old.

In 1989, Eliezer and I bought a parcel of land in Ra'anana on Hashirion Street and built two private homes next to each other. We moved to our current home in the Kiryat Ganim neighborhood twenty-four years ago. Zeev and his wife, Yafit, live next door. Their two daughters live in Ra'anana, and their son lives in the nearby community of Tel Mond. I have three grandchildren and I am blessed with six great-grandchildren.

Mark family today in Israel.

Mordechai and Yehudit with their son Zeev, 2017.

Chapter Four

Walking Tall

Frida Solomon Katz

My name is Frida Solomon Katz. I was born on January 9, 1932, in the town of Burdujeni, Romania, which was part of Suceava. My parents were born in the same town. My father, Max, was born in 1903; my mother, Chaya, was born in 1904. My brother, Binyamin (Beno), was born in 1929.

My father came from a large family of five brothers and two sisters. My parents were married in 1928. My grandmother lived with one of her sons, daughter-in-law and their five children. At home, my parents spoke Yiddish, but Romanian was our mother tongue and everyday language. We owned a four-room house that was situated on a large tract of land.

We were religious, but only the rabbi in our town had payot. The town had a kosher butcher. Every Shabbat I went to synagogue with my father. I remember that once I wore a blouse that was tied with laces on the bodice, and the rabbi told me to go home and change into something more conservative. Before Shabbat, I would go to my grandmother's home to wish her "Shabbat Shalom." On Friday nights, my mother would remove a small piece of dough from the challah to make a blessing for our family, the "Hafrashat Challah."

My father had a store in the center of town that sold grains of wheat. By 1940, the Romanian government aligned with the Nazis, and they took my father's store away. From 1939 to 1941, we had no source of income and our life was in a downward trajectory.

Even though there were Jews and gentiles in my town, all my friends were Jewish. We would walk in the countryside—not everyone owned horses. There was always an element of antisemitism. I started school at five years of age, and due to WWII, I only completed second grade, which was when our school principal said that Jews could not attend school. As anti-Jewish sentiment grew, the Romanian children would call the Jews "Legionarim," which means "legions" or "growth."

In 1940, I was seven and a half years old. My memories are faint, but my personal accounts are still vivid. In 1940, on the eve of Simchat Torah, the Nazis and Romanians came to our town. We were given three hours to gather all our belongings and turn over the house keys to the city officials. One of the government officials played a drum to announce to the villagers the Nazis were coming. We were not told anything, and our food was still in the oven. We were only told to meet at the train station to go to Transnistria.

Transnistria was a large regional area that is part of the Moldavian Republic, which occupies a narrow strip of land between the Dniester River that is Ukraine and part of Moldova. In 1924, Transnistria became an autonomous political entity. The Romanian administration of Transnistria attempted to stabilize the situation in the area under Romanian control. During the Romanian occupation from 1941–44, between 150,000 and 250,000 Ukrainian and Romanian Jews were deported to Transnistria. The majority were executed or died from other causes in ghettos and concentration camps of the Governorate.

Our family, including my cousins and grandmother, boarded the cattle car. We were not given any food or water and had to stay on the train without being able to go out to relieve ourselves, so you can imagine the smell. After traveling all night, we arrived in Bessarabia, Ukraine. There, we met other Jews from Europe at the synagogue.

Bessarabia is a region in Eastern Europe bounded by the Dniester River on the east and the Prut River on the west. About two-thirds of Bessarabia lies within modern-day Moldova. The Ukrainian Budjak region covers the southern coastal region, and part of the Ukrainian *Chernivtsi Oblast* covers a small area in the north. In 1940, the Soviet Union pressured Romania to withdraw from Bessarabia, allowing Russia to annex the region.

We left Bessarabia, traveling on wooden rafts toward Mohyliv. Before we entered the rafts, we turned over all our jewelry and gold to the Ukrainians and Germans. There were too many of us on the rafts, making it too dangerous. The Nazis threw people from the raft, and they drowned. In the morning, we arrived in Mohyliv and were taken to a large school.

Mohyliv-Podilskyi is a city in Ukraine located in the historic region of Podolia, on the border with Bessarabia, Moldova, along the left bank of the Dniester River. On the opposite side of the river lies the Moldovan town of Otaci. The two municipalities are connected by a bridge. Mohyliv-Podilskyi was occupied by Romanian and German troops in July 1941 and incorporated into the Romanian-ruled Transnistria Governorate. Soon thereafter, thousands of Jews in the town were murdered by the occupiers.

Mohyliv-Podilskyi soon became a transit camp for Jews expelled from Bessarabia and Bukovina to Transnistria. From September 1941 to February 1942, more than 55,000 deportees came through the town. Thousands of people were jammed into the transit camp and were treated cruelly by Romanian guards. Thousands of Jews were forced to travel by foot to nearby towns and villages.

After we arrived in Mohyliv-Podilskyi, we traveled by foot some ten kilometers per day. From Mohyliv-Podilskyi, we continued to walk to Lysychansk, Ukraine. After two days, my grandmother and my uncle Ephraim, the youngest one, died along the way. Others died as well from exhaustion and malnutrition. We wanted to dig a grave for them, but the Nazis refused. We walked for weeks. Not only did we lack food and water, but we were not allowed to change our clothes. Out of desperation, we traded our clothes for food. En route, we slept on the dirt floors of small storage houses used by farmers, where they crammed forty to forty-five people into one room. It was winter and freezing cold, and there were no blankets.

My father devised an escape plan. One night when the Nazi guards were asleep, my parents, my brother, my uncle Ramiel, and I snuck out quietly. We succeeded to get past the guards, and we walked through the forests back to Mohyliv-Podilskyi. It was 1941. It took us weeks to get there. On the way, my uncle died.

When we arrived in Mohyliv-Podilskyi, we went to the synagogue, and they found us a Jewish family in the ghetto to live with. We stayed with them for two years. In Mohyliv-Podilskyi there were Nazis and Ukrainians. Ephraim's five children died from lice bites during those two years in Lysychansk. We were starving and infested with lice. My father and brother worked on the construction of a bridge.

We had one experience that almost cost us our lives. My three-year-old cousin was outside looking for his cousin Cherbo. A Nazi soldier came up to him with his big fierce dog and started speaking to him in German. My cousin didn't understand German and only spoke Romanian. It so happens that my little cousin Cherbo was hiding in the closet. The soldier became flustered and confused, so he gave up and walked away.

In December 1943, there were over 3,000 Jews who could return to Romania, and in March 1944 Jewish leaders in Bucharest received permission to bring back 1,400 orphans. Those who stayed were killed by German bombs. Most of the deportees could return to Romania in the spring of 1945.

At the end of WWII, the Russians took over, and they enlisted my father in the Red Army. He served in the army for three years. We never saw him or spoke with him during that time. My brother was too young to enlist.

After two years in Mohyliv-Podilskyi, my mother, brother, and I returned to Bessarabia by horse carriage, with the permission of the Russians because my father was in the Red Army. We stayed in Bessarabia for a year. I worked with my mother knitting sweaters for non-Jewish families with whom we lived. We moved around a lot and stayed with a different family every week without having to pay.

We left Bessarabia by train and went back to Botoşani, Romania, to my maternal grandmother's old house. The Russians had taken over Romania. We stayed there for a short time. Botoşani had a large Jewish community established during the seventeenth century. It was the second largest and most important city in Moldavia until the end of the nineteenth century. During WWII, on April 7, 1944, Botoşani was captured by Soviet troops of the Second Ukrainian Front during the Uman–Botoşani Offensive.

We left my grandmother's home and took a train to Burdujeni, which was forty kilometers away. It was 1945, and I was thirteen years old. Our home was in disarray from the war. The interior of the house had been used as a horse stable. We repaired the house. I went back to school and completed eighth grade. A few Jews who had returned to our town. The synagogue remained intact, as well as the kosher butcher shop. I lived there until I was twenty-one.

Romania was under communist rule, so the economic situation was very depressing. The Romanian government had antisemitic views. My father returned to Burdujeni in 1946 after having served in the Red Army for three years, and we were finally reunited.

In July 1941, thousands of Jews from towns and villages throughout the county were forcibly moved to Suceava. There were then 5,874 Jews living in the county, of whom 3,523 lived in the town itself. Jews from several streets were deported to Transnistria on October 8, 1941, in a transport that included residents of Burdujeni and Iţcani. Two additional freight cars carried the remainder of Suceava's Jews to Mohyliv-Podilskyi. After the deportations, thirty-one Jews were left in the county, of whom twenty-seven lived in the town.

In 1944, when the surviving deportees returned, the number of Jews of Suceava reached approximately 4,000, as many Jews from northern Bucovina chose to settle in the Romanian part of the province. The community was reestablished. During the first years of the communist regime, its leadership was assumed by the Jewish Democrat Committee. Jewish schools were nationalized in 1948; however, the teaching of Yiddish was maintained in only a few of them. Later, the community organized courses in Hebrew. The number of Jews ultimately decreased as a result of emigration.

In 1953, I was twenty-one. My cousin who lived in Bucharest invited me to a wedding. Her husband had a cousin named Mandel Katz. At the wedding, my aunt introduced me to Mandel, who was twenty-eight. After three days, Mandel and I were engaged. We were married on December 20, 1953. Rabbi Rosen, a well-known rabbi, married us in Bucharest.

Frida and Mandel's wedding in Romania.

Mandel was religious and worked as an accountant at a factory. We lived in Bucharest for eight years in a one-room rented apartment. Mandel had two brothers and a sister. On March 4, 1958, Cornel, our fist son, was born.

In 1961, Mandel and I decided to make aliya. Cornel was three years old. We took a train to Italy. From there, we took a ship to Israel called the *Hermes*, organized by the Jewish Agency. It took us a week to reach Israel.

When we landed at the Haifa port, we were met by Mandel's sister, Chana, who had made aliya with her husband in 1950. They lived in Givatayim on a street called Derech Hashalom. They had a little girl, and ten years later they had another girl. Chana's husband was Romanian. We stayed with them for three months. The government gave us a small apartment in Herzliya, on Weizmann Street, called Shikun Weizmann.

Katz family.

My mother and my brother made aliya in 1964. They started out living in the south close to Ashdod, then moved to Herzliya to be with us. My mother lived with us until her death in 1979, at the age of 75. Beno was married in Romania and had one son. He died at the age of seventy. Beno's son, Zvi, lives in Rishon Lezion and works as a taxi driver. My husband died in 2013. My son Cornel lives in Rishon Lezion and is an accountant. His two daughters were born in Israel. Noam is twenty-seven, married and lives in Manhattan, where she is studying to be an opera singer. Yael, twenty-three, lives in Herzliya and is studying at Tel Aviv University.

Frida and Mandel in their early years in Israel.

Mandel and Frida with their grandchildren Yael and Noam.

Chapter Five

From Hungary to Haifa: A Harrowing Journey

Chana Friedman Fishlovitch

My name is (Morgid) Chana Friedman Fishlovitch (in Hungary we were required to have a Hungarian first name as well). I was born on February 22, 1925, in the town of Kiskunmajsa, Hungary. I was the second of seven siblings. My eldest sister, Irena Pnina, was born in 1923. Asher was born in 1927; later that year, Yossi was born; Dov was born in 1929; Ilana was born in 1931; and Zippora, the youngest by fourteen years, was born in 1939.

My father, Shmuel, and my mother, Frida, were born in Hajdúnánás, which was 207 kilometers from Budapest. After they married, they moved to Kiskunmajsa because my father obtained work there. My mother came from a family of six children. Her sister had two children.

Chana, 7-years old, 1945.

We were a religious family. However, because there were so few Jews in our town and certainly no Jewish schools, I studied at the Roman Catholic church. I managed to complete four grades and was one of the best students in my class. There were only two other Jews in my school, and I was friends with one of them. The principal, who was the priest, decided which pupils would continue to study. Of course, my being Jewish was used against me, and he decided I could not study any further. His decision was in line with the Numerous Clausus Law. Under that law, the Hungarian government limited the number of Jewish students who were permitted to study—a religious or racial quota.

I remember going to a friend's house who was not Jewish, and her brother told me to leave because he didn't want Jews in their house. Clearly there was a strong presence of antisemitism, and the Roman Catholic Church was notably the worst. The Hungarians said that Jews were hungry wolves who killed Jesus Christ. Close to the outbreak of WWII, antisemitism increased in Hungary. Some Hungarians broke the windows of my father's shop.

In 1929, we moved to Hajdúnánás, a small town in the Hajdu district in eastern Hungary, 38 kilometers from Debrecen. Jews were not allowed to settle in the town until the middle of the nineteenth century. Relations between the residents of the town and the Jews were normal. Like in Kiskunhalas, the period of the White Terror lasted from 1919-1921 and was a difficult time for Jews. The White Terror was a counter-revolutionary movement, aiming to crush Hungary's Soviet governmental influence over Hungarians. Even though many of the victims were Jewish, local authorities did their best to protect Jews. Despite this, a few Jews were expelled and by 1920, only 1,147 Jews lived in Hajdúnánás.

We had a Jewish school with a gymnasium. Because we were Jewish, we had to apply to get accepted to the school. I was able to study for three more years at a technical school until I was thirteen years old.

My parents couldn't afford to purchase a home, so we rented one. As I said, my family was religious. We observed Shabbat to the letter. My mother would not even use a broom to sweep the floor on Shabbat. There was a synagogue and a kosher butcher. My father went to synagogue every day and prayed with tefillin. On Yom Kippur, he performed a ritual sacrifice (*kapparot*), where a rabbi waved a live chicken over his head. The Jews in the town were generally not religious, and the Old Testament was written in both Hungarian and Hebrew. Men wore hats, not kippot. A bakery would cook our food for Shabbat, including the challah. We gave them the dough with which to bake the ritual bread. The baker closed his shop at noon for Shabbat.

In Hajdúnánás, my father opened a shop in the center of town, where he sold fabric. Every three months, there was an open market in Debrecen to purchase textiles. Next to his shop was my grandmother's clothing store. My father was a good businessman and was able to sell his stock quite quickly. There was another shop that sold expensive items, but they always had difficulty selling their merchandise. When customers didn't have money, my father would trade material for food. During WWII, it was difficult for my father to buy quality textiles. My mother insisted that I work at my grandfather's fabric store as a seamstress.

Debrecen is Hungary's second largest city after Bucharest. It is the seat of Hajdu-Bihar county. It was the largest Hungarian city in the eighteenth century and was an important cultural center. In 1814, about 120 Jews settled in Debrecen. Twenty years later, Jews could purchase real estate. By 1919, Jews represented 10% of the population, with more than 10,000 who owned almost half of the large properties in and around the town. However, the Hungarian antisemitic laws of 1938 caused many businesses to close.

In 1940, there were 12,000 Jews in Debrecen. In 1941, the number of Jews decreased to 9,142. On March 30, 1944 (a week before Passover), Jews were ordered to wear the yellow Star of David. Cars were confiscated, and phone lines were cut. During the week of Passover, many Jewish dignitaries were taken to a nearby prison camp. The number of prisoners reached 300. A week later, all Jewish stores were closed, and there was a public burning of Jewish books. On April 28, 1944, the Jews were forced to build a ghetto.

In 1944, the Nazis and the Hungarians launched an attack against the Jews. In Hajdúnánás, we were told to go to the backyard of the synagogue. My grandparents were in their mid-sixties, and I was nineteen years old. There was a lack of communication among the Jews in our community. My father had a daily Hungarian newspaper, but that didn't tell us much. Only from the synagogue did we hear things. The Germans and their Hungarian counterparts told us to deposit our gold and jewelry at the bank and keep the receipt. I did not deposit my mother's wedding ring.

Our entire family, except for my father and grandparents, were told to go to the train station. Once all the Jews were gathered at the synagogue in Hajdúnánás, we were told to walk to the train station. The trains arrived, and we boarded the cattle cars. There were about eighty people in each rail car. We stood for the entire time. The train was traveling to Vienna. There was no water or food and only a small window. The pungent stench stifled the air. People became sick. We made our first stop in Debrecen to gather more Jews. When the doors opened, many Jews had already died from starvation and sickness.

Chana's father's family in Hungary before the war.

On the way to Vienna the train made several stops, and my brothers Yossi and Asher were sent to other camps. But the rest of our family remained together.

When we arrived in Vienna, we heard bombing from the Americans and the British. We were moved to a hut in the center of the city. They packed more than thirty-five of us into a small room, one on top of another. We were assigned work to help the Germans build an explosives factory. Many of the Jewish men worked in manual labor building the facility with cement and raw materials. The work conditions were considered acceptable. To get to the factory, we took an electric train. Our hut was close to the central train station. Our bosses at the factory were French and Czech engineers who were kind people. They even gave us Hungarian newspapers to read.

Our food staple was two pieces of bread and pork soup. There were two bakeries nearby. I collected bread and put it under my bed. One day, as a friend and I were sitting in a Viennese café, a German officer saw us and gave the owner fifty German marks to cover our bill. But when he found out that we were two Jewish girls, he gave him another fifty marks. The owner used the money to buy us potatoes. We boiled the potatoes and had a nice meal. In Vienna, gentiles who saw us on the street knew we were Jewish. They felt sorry for us and gave us small change.

Asher (brother) and Hoynon (wife) at the Cyprus Detention camp.

My sister Irena was part of a group that worked on the roofs of apartment buildings, fixing broken shingles. From her vantage point, she saw Russians shooting at people. One day while on the roof, she was shot. A gentile Austrian woman from the building took her to an SS hospital until she was in stable condition. After my sister was released, she stayed in the home of that kind woman.

During bombing raids, the German Red Cross forbade the Jews to enter the bomb shelters.

The war was reaching its end, and the Germans feared that they would not be able fulfill their goal of killing all the Jews—Hitler's Final Solution. In December 1944, the Germans told us that we had to walk to the Mauthausen concentration camp, which was 166 kilometers away. That was insane. With me were my mother, my brother Dov and my sisters Zippora and Irena. Zippora was five years old. I was nineteen.

The Nazis made us walk day and night. I carried Zippora in my arms during the entire trip. Every two kilometers, the guards would change. To add insult to injury, they beat us. This was not a slow march but a race to the finish line. We were given little to no food or water. Many people died along the way.

Near the end of the war, when Germany's military force was collapsing, the Allied armies closed in on the Nazi concentration camps. The Soviets approached from the east, and the British, French, and Americans came from the west. The Germans frantically began to move the prisoners out of the camps near the front and took them to be used as forced laborers in camps inside Germany. Prisoners were first taken by train and then by foot on "death marches," as they became known.

Prisoners were forced to march long distances in bitter cold, with little or no food, water, or rest. Those who couldn't keep up were shot. The largest death marches took place in the winter of 1944 to 1945, when the Soviet army began its liberation of Poland. Nine days before the Soviets arrived at Auschwitz, the Germans marched tens of thousands of prisoners out of the camp toward Wodzisław, a town thirty-five miles away, where they were put on freight trains bound for other camps. About one in four people died on the way.

The Nazis often killed large groups of prisoners before, during or after the marches. During one march, 7,000 Jewish prisoners, 6,000 of them women, were moved from camps in the Danzig region, which was bordered on the north by the Baltic Sea. On the ten-day march, 700 people were murdered. Those who were still alive when the marchers reached the shores of the sea were driven into the water and shot.

We finally arrived at Mauthausen after a grueling trip. When we arrived, the guards told us to stand in lines and continued to beat us until they received their next orders. Mauthausen was notorious for its crematorium (gas chambers). There were large tents for the prisoners. The Americans and the Russians were on their way. The Germans were in despair, as time was against them before their Final Solution plan could become a reality.

Words cannot describe the carnage we observed. There were mountains of bodies, bones, and skin. The odor permeated the camp. The rancid stench of death will never be forgotten. We had to dig graves for the dead. Lice killed people, and many prisoners contracted typhus, like Zippora. We remained in Mauthausen for six months until its final liberation.

Mauthausen was one of the most notorious Nazi concentration camps. It was located near the village of Mauthausen on the Danube River, twelve miles (twenty kilometers) east of Linz, Austria. It was established in April 1938. About 200,000 prisoners passed through Mauthausen. Some 120,000 of them died, mainly from starvation, disease, and the hardships of slave labor. About 38,000 of the dead were Jews. From April 1944 to January 1945, many Jews were gassed to death. The SS fled Mauthausen shortly before American troops entered the camp on May 5, 1945.

The camp provided labor to work at the abandoned stone quarries nearby. During its first year, the camp received prisoners transferred from Dachau, mainly convicted criminals, but also so-called "asocial elements," which included political prisoners, homosexuals, and others. The camp later became a detention center for anti-Nazis from all over Europe, including 10,000 Spanish Republicans. In November 1941, Soviet prisoners of war began arriving. The first Jews arrived in May 1941, but Jews were a small minority of the camp prisoners until 1944, when Jews from Poland and Hungary came in masses. Later, Mauthausen absorbed survivors of the infamous death marches from evacuated extermination camps.

All categories of prisoners and inmates were starved, beaten, used for medical experiments and subjected to the most grueling work, especially in the local quarries. The Nazis delivered unruly prisoners and captured escapees from other camps to Mauthausen for punishment by beating, hard labor, shooting, or gassing.

The Russians finally arrived from Vienna, and the Americans from the direction of Mauthausen. The crematoriums were closed. We stayed in the villas of the SS soldiers. The Red Cross fed us sardines and other food. When the Americans arrived, they had doctors look after us. We were malnourished, starving, and our stomachs had shrunk. We were skin and bones. When the prisoners saw food, they immediately ate whatever they were given. Many died due to diarrhea and other related disorders. When we were liberated, we were weak and sick. We heard stories from the other Jewish prisoners about what they had witnessed in the other Nazi death camps.

At last, we returned to our hometown of Hajdúnánás by train. The passengers were half-dead, malnourished, starving with sickness, barely holding on. The train stopped in Debrecen, then went on to Hajdúnánás. My brothers Yossi and Asher were already back home. My sister Irena had yet to recover from her bullet wound. She was found by the JOINT (American Joint Distribution Committee) and was returned home. I was sick with lice.

Before making aliya, my mother, brother Dov and my sisters Zippora and Irena spent a year in Pocking, Germany. With the assistance of the Jewish Agency of Israel, we took a train to Camerano, Italy. Then we boarded a ship for Israel. We arrived in Israel on January 1, 1948 and landed in Nahariya. The crew took us by raft to the shore.

Chana (second from the left, sitting) with friends at Pocking DP camp in Germany after the war; she she lived there for one year.

When the ship approached the port, the British didn't give us permission to enter Palestine because we didn't have legal documents. So, the captain took us ashore, and some of the passengers were taken by the British. But I managed to escape with the assistance of the Hagana organization.

Once we landed, some of the passengers went to Kiryat Shmuel and others to various kibbutzim and moshavim. I was taken to Kfar Ata near Haifa. It was a temporary camp for new immigrants. I stayed there for a short time. Then I was told to go to Beit Haluzot in Ra'anana. While waiting there for a bus, I met a man from Hajdúnánás who by chance turned out to be a cousin on my mother's side. He took me to his home in Haifa. He worked in a bakery, and I worked there as well.

Chana's parents Israel and Frida with her brothers Eran, Yossi, Tobi. 1947, Israel.

Chana.

Chana in Israel.

My brother Asher got married in Cyprus at the internment camp and later came to Israel. The War of Independence broke out, and Yossi enlisted. Because he was married, he was given a small apartment in Kiryat Tivon by the Jewish Agency. In Kiryat Tivon, I met a man from Germany who owned a small grocery store, and I worked for him. During that time, I continued to live in Haifa with my cousin.

Israel was just a young country and was in difficult economic conditions. Food was rationed under strict controls. Each person was issued a card with which to purchase food.

I rented a small apartment in Kiryat Amal, then moved to an Arab neighborhood in Tel Chanan. It was a low-income area, and the apartment was in terrible condition. When my mother arrived, she stayed with me.

Chana's brother Yossi with his wife Nitza in Israel.

I met a man from the store in Kiryat Tivon who was Hungarian. He lived in a small apartment in Haifa with three other men. He got married and bought an apartment in Kiryat Tivon. He introduced me to his good friend Shmuel Fishlovitch, who was a survivor from Bekescsaba, Hungary.

Shmuel lost his entire family in the war. They had once been a wealthy family who were in the textile business and owned a large house. I was twenty-seven years old when I met Shmuel, who was two years older than me. After he and I dated for a year and a half, we were married in 1954. We then moved to a small apartment in Haifa.

Chana and Shmuel Fishlovitz.

Chana's family at her wedding.

Shmuel worked for an oil refinery, and I continued to work in the grocery store in Kiryat Tivon. Our first son, Moshe, was born in Haifa in

1955. In 1958, we purchased a small single-story house in Kiryat Tivon. In 1960, our daughter Aviva was born.

In 1970, we expanded our home to accommodate our family. Shmuel and I slept in the living room, and Moshe and Aviva had separate rooms. The grocery store closed in 1970. I then worked as a kindergarten teacher in Kiryat Tivon for the next twelve years. Shmuel continued to work for the oil company at an administrative level. He retired at age sixty-five. Shmuel died in 2008. After my husband's death, I sold our home and moved to Hod Hasharon.

Moshe is single and lives in Tel Aviv, where he manufactures clothing. Aviva got married in 1992 and lives in Hod Hasharon. She has two daughters, of twenty-three and twenty-six. Both are students.

My Family after the War

My parents lived in Tel Hanan, then moved to Haifa. My mother died at age ninety-four, and my father at eighty-five.

My sister Irena (Pnina) Sheinberger got married and moved to Israel. She had two sons—Ephraim and Arya (who died in Israel). She passed away.

My brother Asher Friedman got married in Cyprus, then moved to Israel. He had two daughters—Hedva and Dina. He passed away.

My brother Joseph (Yossi) Friedman got married in Israel. He had three sons—Ron, Assaf, and Amir. He passed away.

My brother Beru (Dov) Friedman was married in Israel. He has three children—Menachem, Miriam, and Zvi.

My sister Hindu (Ilana) Katz got married in Israel. She has three children—Sarah, Dina, and Samuel.

My sister Tuby (Zippora) got married in Israel. She has six children—Isaac, Haya, Mordechai, Mary, Ephraim, and Aryeh.

Chapter Six

Denmark Defies Nazis

Robert (Reuven) Fischermann

I, Robert (Reuven) Fischermann, was born on April 19, 1928, in Copenhagen, Denmark. I am one of six children. My eldest sister, Fanny, was born in 1923, followed by my brother Ante, born in 1925; my brother Salle was born in 1929; my sister Rebekka, who suffered from epilepsy, was born in 1932; and my youngest brother, Mogens, was born in 1938.

It took me sixty-three years before I was able to share my experiences as a survivor of the Theresienstadt concentration camp in Czechoslovakia, where I spent a period of eighteen grueling months. My family, excluding my father and one brother, survived, and now I am proud to tell my story to ensure that this tragedy never happens again.

My parents met at a social event organized by the Jewish community and were married by the chief rabbi, Max Friediger, on January 21, 1923. My father was twenty-nine years old.

My maternal grandfather, Meir Wygodzki, was born in Poland in 1854 and worked as a tailor. My grandmother, Ruda Moszkowicz, was eight years younger. They married in 1882. They were Orthodox Jews and had five children: Leon, Elias, Malka, Fanny, and Itzak, who were born between 1884 and 1897.

My mother, Malka, was born in 1895 in Kalisz in the province of Poznan, Poland. During the farmers' rebellion in 1905 against the Russians, many people were forced to escape, including Jews. My mother's family fled Poland together with her brothers, Elias and Leon. They sought refuge in Denmark together with most of my mother's family. They first fled to Sweden, then to Denmark—without passports.

Robert's mother Malka in Denmark after the war.

My father, Elias Leopold Fischermann, was born on August 8, 1894, in the town of Frauenburg, now called Saldus, in western Latvia. I have fond memories of him as a loving father. His eldest brother, Salomon, moved to America, and I lost contact with him. I estimate that my father, his mother, and brothers arrived in Denmark in 1912. My father with his two brothers planned to work in Denmark and then move to America when they'd earned enough money. I don't know the fate of my grandfather, Anzelim Moscha Fischermann. My grandmother, Mera Brandt, lived with us in Copenhagen and died in 1932 when I was four years old.

My parents almost never spoke about their journey to Denmark. Only after living in Denmark for many years did they receive Danish citizenship.

My father was eighteen years old when he arrived in Denmark. He began an apprenticeship with a Jewish entrepreneur painter who had a workshop in Nytorv, Copenhagen. Painting jobs were sporadic, so at times my father was out of work, which had a significant impact on our family's ability to pay the bills. My father said he began to work when he was twelve years old. He lacked good negotiating skills, which had a negative effect on his ability to earn a proper living. There were times when we could not afford to pay the rent on our apartment. My father worked on Shabbat, so my mother's family thought he was not Jewish.

My mother took care of our household finances and "wore the pants" in our family. For example, she sublet a room in our apartment to earn extra money. When she took us to the market at Nørrebro Station with the shopping trolley, she bargained with the merchants.

I started to work at age twelve to earn pocket money by delivering milk and bread to customers. I began work at 6 a.m. earning two Danish kroner per week. The children I grew up with knew I was Jewish and saw me as different. I don't think they even knew what it meant, but they attacked me for being a Jew.

We rented our first apartment at 3 Revalsgade Street in the Vesterbro area of Copenhagen, a Jewish neighborhood where many immigrants lived. The neighborhood was considered low-income. Our family was traditional in regard to religion. We observed the Jewish holidays but did not fast on Yom Kippur and drove on Shabbat. Later we moved to Hothers Plads near Nørrebro Station, where the conditions were better. After that, we moved to the district of Bispebjerg.

Robert's father Elias Leopold Fischermann.

Many of the Jews in Copenhagen lived in the neighborhoods of Borgergade, Adelgade, Westerbro, and Nørrebro, which were considered slum neighborhoods. Many Jewish immigrants worked as tailors, shoemakers or painters for low wages, under poor working conditions. Some traveled around the country as day laborers.

Several Jewish families lived in Hothers Plads, where my parents had friends. One time my father lost his entire week's salary at a card game, causing severe family stress because we were dependent on his earnings.

My mother's brother Leon and her sister Fega both died on January 21, 1919, from the Spanish flu. The next day, her brother Elias died as well. They are buried in the Mosaic Cemetery in Copenhagen. When Leon died, his wife, Debora, was pregnant.

My parents spoke Yiddish among their Jewish friends. They managed to pick up the Danish language, but my mother was not as fluent as my father, so she was more dependent on him when it came to communication.

I went to a Jewish elementary school and completed seventh grade. Starting work at 6 a.m. and then running off to school made me tired, so my grades were not that good. The principal, who was not Jewish, did not recommend that I continue my studies.

On April 9, 1940, the Germans occupied Denmark. For three and a half years there was no persecution of Danish Jews. In 1943, we moved to a new apartment, and I started middle school. It was a public school for children of all faiths. I was one of the top pupils. Among the subjects they taught us were carpentry and garden landscaping. I had an affinity for carpentry, but my father didn't want me to be a carpenter.

The welfare of the Danish Jews was of great importance to the king of Denmark, Christian X, and the Danish citizens. The Germans ordered the Jews in Denmark to wear armbands with the yellow Star of David. In defiance, King Christian X of Denmark (1912 to 1947) told the Germans that he and the Danish people would wear the Jewish armband as well. The Germans then removed the mandate for Jews to wear the armband.

Until the end of August 1943, there was no persecution of Jews in Denmark. Nazi Germany considered the Danes as Aryans like themselves. During the war, Germany depended on Denmark's farming industry for food, and that was one of the major reasons that Denmark was not attacked like other European countries.

My cousin Sara lived in Norway and had two young children. When the Germans deported Norwegian Jews, they took only the men and the older children. Sara remained with her two little children. Her husband, Jack, was sent to Auschwitz, and she never saw him again.

On September 17, 1943, the office of the Jewish community in Ny Kongensgade was ransacked. A few weeks earlier, files from the office, including lists of the members' addresses, were confiscated, which gave the Germans personal information on the Jews. On September 28, 1943, a German attaché, Georg Duckwitz, who worked in the German embassy, warned leading Danish politicians about Germany's action against Denmark's Jews and informed the Jewish community.

In September 1943, two days before Rosh Hashana, the chief rabbi, Marcus Melchior, warned Copenhagen's Jewish community that German occupation forces were preparing an extensive action against the Jews. Rabbi Melchior replaced the previous chief rabbi, Max Friediger, who was arrested by the Germans and was interned in the Horserød camp. Members of the Jewish community warned us against celebrating Rosh Hashana at home to avoid being arrested. Danes who were gentiles hid the Jews from the Nazis. They were opposed to persecution and antisemitism. We went to stay at the home of some Christian friends.

During the night, my sister Rebekka had a serious epilepsy attack, and my father decided to go home and call a doctor. That was very fateful.

At five o' clock in the morning on Saturday, October 2, 1943, the day after Rosh Hashana, the German police came to the house. There were five armed Germans and one Danish collaborator. My younger brother Salle and I were sleeping in the same bed. We rushed into the dining room. My father was already getting dressed.

When we heard the Germans banging on the door of our apartment, our first thought was to help our father escape. Salle and I ran into the bedroom to find sheets. We tied them together and secured them to the railing of our fourth-floor balcony which faced the other side of the street. My father started climbing down. As we opened the front door, five armed German soldiers rushed into the apartment with a Danish collaborator and noticed that my father had escaped via the balcony.

One of the soldiers sent two others to find my father and ordered them to shoot him if they found him and he tried to flee. They took my brother to identify my father and told us to take our belongings. The soldiers left our apartment door open, and our neighbors stole everything.

We thought that the Germans would be looking for my father and my older siblings Fanny and Ante. However, Fanny and Ante were already in hiding. My mother, younger brother Salle, Rebekka and Mogens, who was five, thought we were safe and did not expect to be arrested by the occupation forces.

From left to right: mother, Robert, Salle, Fanny, Ante, father, and Rebekka.

Robert's father Leopold with his sister Rebekka.

On September 18, 1943, Rolf Günther, head of a special commando force, was ordered to send Denmark's Jews to the concentration camps. About 500 Jews boarded the *Wärteland* anchored in Copenhagen, which set sail for Germany.

Danish clergymen, civil servants, doctors, store owners, farmers, fishermen, and teachers protected the Jews. Christian families, priests, and doctors helped save the 7,000 remaining Jews. A United Lutheran Church openly and persistently challenged the German offensive. Many Torahs from Rabbi Melchior's synagogue were hidden in the crypt of Trinity Church. Dr. Koster, who oversaw the Bispebjerg Hospital, was instrumental in arranging for hundreds of Danish Jews to be hidden in the hospital before they made their escape to Sweden. The psychiatric building and the nurses' quarters were filled with Jewish refugees, who were fed from the hospital's kitchen. Virtually the entire medical staff of the hospital cooperated to save Jewish lives. Once it became known among Danes what the hospital was doing, money was donated from all over the country.

Many refugees were driven to the coast in the hospital's ambulances to make their escape. Local fishermen were paid money to help transport Jews to Sweden. Many completed the two-mile boat trip successfully without being intercepted by German patrol rowboats.

The details of my nineteen-year-old sister Fanny's escape to Sweden helped me form a clearer picture of the fate of my family. My parents had no money to give to those who assisted the Jews for passage to cross into Sweden. The fishermen, who used their fishing boats, demanded a lot of money for the dangerous trip. My uncle, who was a butcher, had sent one of his employees to us with 15,000 Danish kroner. That was a large sum, but the young man never arrived.

While Fanny was packing her things, my father and my brother Ante arrived at the factory where she worked, seeking to escape, despite their lack of cash. Father limped because of the pain he had sustained from the fall during his escape from our apartment. Passing the synagogue in Krystalgade, they saw Germans and hurried to the train station. They went with many other Danish Jews toward the coast of North Zeeland. Fanny's boss had given them the key to his house in Ordrup. He tried to persuade my father to wait a couple of days to feel better before they continued to Sweden. My three family members arrived in Snekkersten and found shelter with a priest's family. Fanny, Ante, and my father headed for Gilleleje because they had heard it was a safe hiding place and it might be possible to get to Sweden from there. The name of the Gestapo's Danish envoy in the area was Juhl. Nicknamed "Gestapo Juhl," he worked as a driver for Heinrich Himmler. At a church, the Gestapo demanded the keys to the church, but the priest refused. This aroused suspicion, so Juhl and his men made a thorough check and found sixty-nine Jews seeking to escape to Sweden.

My father, Fanny, and Ante returned to Egebæksvang. Helped by some Danish volunteers, they were hidden in a hay loft. It was there that they met Dr. Jørgen Gersfelt. He examined my father and diagnosed him with two broken ribs and a fractured knee. In trying to escape from our apartment, my father had reached only one floor sliding down the sheets that Salle and I had tied together. Instead of slowly descending safely, he had fallen two floors onto hard stones.

My father was in severe pain but fully determined to escape to Sweden with my two siblings. That evening, Fanny, Ante, and my father were brought to a dentist's house in Snekkersten, while seven other Jews arrived. One of them was Bruno Schmitz, a young Jew from Germany, a *halutz* (the Hebrew word for young Jews on their way to Palestine). Bruno was the only survivor from the church raid in Gilleleje. He had evaded the Gestapo by climbing the church tower and hiding behind the bells.

The other 69 Jews were arrested. The Jews who found refuge at the dentist's house were brother and sister Harry (19) and Sonja (17) Sandler; Dora Thing (24) with her one-year old daughter, Høne; Dora's brother, Leopold Recht (19); and his friend Benjamin Blüdnikow. During the evening, they decided to sail to Sweden. They had a small rowboat, and the Swedish coast was only five kilometers away.

The doctor, Jørgen Gersfelt, came to examine to my father, who was still in pain. He also gave Høne a narcotic injection so that she wouldn't cry during the trip to Sweden. It was suggested that my father should wait a couple of days and that Fanny and Ante should leave. But all three insisted on staying together. The dentist brought them food for the journey.

The fugitives were given a common Danish name. My father was in a great deal of pain and wasn't able to swim. There was no captain. Money had been paid for a fishing boat and a skipper, but they did not arrive. They managed to get hold of a rowboat overloaded with ten passengers, who took turns rowing to the Swedish coast. My father had a tight-fitting towel around his chest, so the rib fracture was no longer bothering him. Dark without wind; the sea was calm. My sister, Ante, and my father sat down in the rowboat with the other passengers.

My father told the crew to row toward the lights to the Swedish coast and follow the stars. The rowboat began to take in water and became too heavy. Water rose until the boat capsized. One-year-old Høne disappeared into the dark deep sea. Leopold dived in, and the infant's body was pulled to the surface. My father disappeared under the rowboat. Ante tried to get him free with an oar, but he failed—so he swam under the rowboat to try to rescue him, and they both drowned.

Bruno also disappeared. Fanny swam around the rowboat with Harry, Sonja, Leopold, and Benjamin. They tried to turn the boat over, but it was too heavy. My sister and Leopold decided to swim back in the ice-cold water to get help.

Two hours later, a Danish sand pumper passed the capsized rowboat and picked up the passengers. Høne's body was stiff and lifeless. The crew picked up the survivors from the capsized rowboat. No one had seen Bruno, my father or my brother after the boat capsized.

Robert's brother Ante.

Fanny and Leopold swam back to Denmark and were washed ashore. Kristian, the dentist's son, found them on the beach. Fanny was unconscious. With help from some fishermen, they too were taken to the Øresunds Hospital. When Fanny regained consciousness, Pastor Dalsager informed her that her father and brother had drowned. The police helped them get to Sweden.

The Germans caught 202 Jews. Three managed to jump out of the train at Roskilde. Between October 13 and November 23, 1943, another 190 Jews were rounded up, raising the total number of Danish Jews arrested to 481.

Immediately after the deportation, various Danish ministries began to gather information about the fate of the Jews. The Danish government requested that the Germans allow Denmark to send food packages to the Jews when the Red Cross representatives or Danish officials made official visits to the concentration camp. The Danish ministries had little knowledge about the camps and were concerned that the Danish Jews would be sent to different camps in Germany and Poland. The state attorney in Denmark and German police chief Werner Best communicated to Nils Svenningse, the head of the Foreign Ministry, that able-bodied Jews would be sent to labor camps in Germany. At the beginning of November 1943, fewer than 500 Danish Jews were sent to the Theresienstadt concentration camp. From the Germans' perspective, the deportation of the Danish Jews was a failed operation. For them, 481 Jews captured out of about 7,500 was an unsatisfactory result. After the war, we were told about an agreement between Germany and Denmark that no Danish Jew would be taken out of Theresienstadt.

In October of 1943, we arrived at the harbor to board the *Wärdeland* ship to Germany. There were five armed Germans and one Danish collaborator. We sailed from the port in Copenhagen to Swinemünde, Germany. We had no food or water. When we arrived in Swinemünde, we were forced into filthy cattle cars at the train station. The dark brown wooden railway cars were locked from the outside, where forty to fifty people were crammed into each car. There were no suitcases, only handbags were allowed with some small items such as shoes, jewelry, and clothes. We stood on the floor side by side. There were fashionable ladies with hats, elderly men, and mothers with children. Only the oldest among us were allowed to sit down.

A tiny beam of light penetrated the small window. A bitter wind blew through cracks, even though the train traveled slowly. The air in the cattle car was suffocating. There was a sharp smell of urine in the blistering cold. One of the women had brought a thermos with water. The water was soon gone, and the woman urinated into the flask. There was an elderly woman who had violently resisted being arrested. The Germans bound her to a mattress and threw her out of the window of her apartment. She was still sitting on the mattress.

We didn't know where the Germans were taking us or how long the journey would last. There was some old straw on the floor, which we moved into a corner and used as a toilet. We were packed together like animals. We stopped in an open landscape for a short toilet break. Men, women, and children defecated next to each other by the railroad tracks, while the armed German soldiers watched us and laughed. That humiliation has haunted me all my life.

Before we were ordered back into the cattle cars, we were given half a loaf of dry bread and a big bucket containing marmalade. It was far from being enough, so the marmalade was quickly devoured. The bucket was used as a new toilet. Some people urinated in their trousers. Others wept. Most of us stood or sat in silence, simply staring into space. We no longer had control of our fate and didn't know what the journey would bring. I was surprised at how quickly life could change from freedom and happiness to total captivity.

At nine o'clock in the evening of October 5, 1943, we arrived at Theresienstadt. We had traveled for 60 hours. When the doors of our cattle car opened, I saw armed Czech gendarmes, and farther away stood the SS officers. One man had died during the journey. He was placed in a wheelbarrow and taken away. The rest of us were ordered into trucks and driven to some barracks outside the camp.

Theresienstadt was a transit camp that held Jews that would later be sent to more brutal camps in the east. The Germans ordered 365 Czech Jews to go to the camp to see if it was functional for 60,000 prisoners and promised them they wouldn't be transferred to concentration camps. The Germans lied, and all the Czech Jews were deported to death camps. The camp could accommodate up to 60,000 Jews from all over Europe, of which 472 were Danish Jews. Over the duration of Theresienstadt, a total of 140,000 Jews passed through the transit camp; they were ultimately transported to death camps.

We were standing in a long line when the SS officers ordered us to answer questions about our financial circumstances and bank account numbers. The details were carefully written down. After that, we underwent a body search. The German officers and the Czech gendarmes confiscated jewelry, money, cigarettes, cosmetics, and watches.

German soldiers handed us yellow Star of David patches and ordered us to put them on our clothes. The gendarmes ordered us to undress. We stood naked, and the hair from all over our bodies was shaved off. We were then disinfected one by one.

Women and children lived in barracks, while the men were accommodated in a stable opposite the barracks. There were bunk beds with no mattresses. The Germans let us keep our clothes, but it was not enough. Later, we learned that we could get clothes from dead prisoners.

A few weeks after our arrival, we were ordered to be ready at four o'clock in the morning. We stood in rows in the barrack yard. On November 11, at exactly at six o'clock, the entire camp population of more than 40,000 people began to leave the camp. The only ones who stayed behind were babies and those who were too sick to walk. We marched in the cold darkness. After two or three kilometers, we were ordered to stand in rows in a valley called Bauschowitzer Kessel. We stood there until late in the evening. At ten p.m., we were ordered to return to the camp.

The first transport to Theresienstadt took place in November 1941, two years before our arrival. It was a task force of 342 young Jewish men, whose task was to turn the town, which had 7,000 inhabitants, to a camp for 60,000 Jews. The 7,000 Czech citizens living in the town were expelled by the Germans.

A wooden wall was built to divide the SS officers from the Jewish population. The officers lived in a four-story building, which was the town's former hotel. About 1,000 Czechoslovakian gendarmes lived close to the SS headquarters, but not together with the Germans. The SS officers formed the Ältesterat, a committee of ten elderly Jewish prisoners who managed and supervised the other prisoners. When the Danish Jews arrived in 1943, there were about 45,000 Jewish prisoners.

The first leader of the Ältesterat was Jakob Edelstein, who was the head of the Jewish community in Prague. He spent three months in Palestine, then returned to Prague to head the Palestine Committee, which helped Jews emigrate to Palestine. He was arrested on November 9, 1943. In December, he was deported to Auschwitz, where he and his family were murdered.

The next leader of the Ältesterat was Paul Epstein, a German sociologist and spokesperson for Jewish organizations in Nazi Germany. Epstein was shot on September 27. Benjamin Murmelstein, a rabbi from Vienna, replaced Epstein as leader of the Ältesterat and remained in that position until May 8, 1945, when the Red Army entered the camp. Murmelstein survived the war.

The camp's Jewish prisoners supplied the German war machine with slave labor. We had various jobs: bakery, military equipment, mines, and mica, which was a heat-resistant material used for gas burners in homes. It was also used by the Nazis for instruments and equipment. My mother worked in the mica mines.

I was a messenger boy and worked for a Czech man who had a certain influence and sometimes gave me a slice of bread. I also worked for an influential Czech couple; the wife was an opera singer.

We had one meal a day, and we each received a card for thirty-one days. Soup was made of potato peels. We received half a loaf of bread per week and some margarine. We stood in line to get the soup.

In 1942, some 16,000 prisoners died. Of the 15,000 children, only about 100 survived. In total, of the 140,000 who arrived in Theresienstadt, 16,832 survived.

We had no communication with the outside world. The only information we obtained was from the stories we heard from other prisoners. No one had detailed information about the death camps.

After a few weeks in quarantine, my family was allotted a room with two other families. The room was about ten meters long and three meters wide. In the back of the room lived the Choleva family with their three children aged between five and thirteen. In the middle lived an elderly couple named Schwartz. And there was my mother with her four children aged between five and fifteen. There were no partitions separating the three families. I spent almost eighteen months in that room. There were wooden beds along an outer wall. The room had an old stove that we used to heat the room and to boil the potatoes that I stole. The other wall faced a yard with a latrine that was divided between men and women. This toilet was a ditch with a board on the top. We were constantly attacked by fleas, lice, and bed bugs. When we woke up in the morning, we were full of bites that itched constantly.

The biggest plague was the itch mites. They crawled under the skin and laid their eggs. They attacked fingers, arms, armpits, chest, and genitals. I was scratching myself all the time, getting large sores. After a while I was placed in medical quarters with other fellow sufferers. After three weeks I was well enough to go back to the family room, only to be attacked again by those horrible mites.

The Jewish administration in the camp was responsible for distributing the scanty ration of bread, that soup made of water and potato skins, soap, and coal for heating in the winter. We had coupons for one portion of food once a day. Sometimes we got a dumpling. We would stand in line with a spoon, fork, and a bowl. We didn't need a knife because there was never any meat. Once a week, each group received a package of margarine and half a loaf of bread per person.

The Germans allowed the Danish prisoners to receive food packages once every six months from their families in Sweden and Denmark. The leader of the Danish Red Cross, Mr. Rosting, did not believe that it was the duty of the Danish Red Cross to send food packages to the Jewish prisoners. Besides the Red Cross, private families in cooperation with the Ministry of Social Affairs and the Foreign Ministry of Denmark sent food packages. Once my sister Fanny knew of our whereabouts, she sent us a food parcel every month from Sweden. At least half the parcels never arrived. They ended up in the hands of German soldiers or the local gendarmes. Even when the parcels did arrive, part of the contents had been looted. One of the most important things we received was vitamin pills. Even with this, there was still not enough to feed us.

Another problem was that some of the Danish Jews were Orthodox and wanted only kosher food. They refused to eat the contents of the parcels, which had a detrimental effect on their health. The Danish chief rabbi, Max Friediger, who arrived in Theresienstadt with us, told the Orthodox Jews that under the circumstances, they had his permission to eat non-kosher food, including pork. Many of those who refused to eat the food in the parcels died of malnutrition.

Of the 472 Danish Jews who arrived in Theresienstadt, fifty-three died, including two of the four babies born between October 1943 and March 1944. Some belonged to a group of Orthodox Jews who refused to eat food from the parcels sent by the Danish Red Cross. Forty-one Danes died of hunger and sicknesses.

In front of the church there was a large open area with a platform where concerts were occasionally performed. Many of the prisoners were artistic personalities; several were very talented musicians. The music was played by a full orchestra under Danish conductor Peter Deutsch. The Nazis would come to listen to the music as well.

There was also theater. The prisoners performed some of Bertolt Brecht's works. My brother Salle worked at the theater. The special children's opera *Brundibar*, written by Czech composer Hans Krasa, was also part of the camp's repertoire. The opera was performed fifty-five times with the permission of the Nazis. About fifty children took part in the performance. The children in the camp were not allowed to study, but some of them received improvised drawing lessons.

When supplies of coal arrived in the camp, Salle, others and I were ordered to unload the coal sacks from the rail cars and carry them along the tracks to a handcart.

I worked in the potato warehouse, where I operated the potato peeling machine. Before the end of the workday, I would steal some potatoes and hide them in my clothes. One day, the woman in charge of the potato peeling told me that she and her husband had been arrested and were placed in the Small Fortress. She was incarcerated in a small dark cell for half a year. She said that when she came out, she couldn't remember her own name. She never saw her husband again.

In December 1943, we heard about the possibility of a visit by the International Swedish and Danish Red Cross. The Germans wanted to convince the Red Cross and the rest of the international community that the imprisonment and persecution of European Jews was carried out in model camps. The Germans postponed the visit of the Red Cross for half a year.

When the Red Cross came, the Danish Jews stood on the road because we were in better health than the other prisoners. We were told not to speak or to say anything negative, otherwise we could be killed or sent eastward to the death camps.

Before the visit, prisoners were assigned to beautify the camp. The buildings had to be repaired and painted. We spread turf and planted flowers. For the first time, benches were placed in the camp, along with playgrounds and sports areas. The dwellings of the more prominent Jews were highlighted as a main attraction and were decorated with furniture, curtains, and flowerpots. A sign on one building read "School," and another sign read "Closed for holiday." But no child in Theresienstadt ever went to school. The school was fake, just like the holiday. Fictitious bakeries and groceries were set up, filled with goods. The Germans printed up special banknotes to give the impression that we went shopping there. On these notes were representations of Moses with the stone tablets of the Ten Commandments. When people from outside sent money to the prisoners, the Germans took the foreign currency and gave them the special camp-money, which was used only to "buy" clothes from dead prisoners.

During the spring of 1943, the German leader of the camp, Karl Rahm, thought the camp was too overcrowded to be shown to the Red Cross. To remedy this, he gave orders to deport more than 17,000 Jewish prisoners. Only one girl from the children's home, a Dane, survived.

On June 23, 1944, the delegation from the International Committee of the Red Cross (ICRC) and two Danish officials arrived at the camp to make an inspection. The participants were Dr. Maurice Rossel, who was from Switzerland, and Danish officials Frants Hvass, chief of the Social Department, and Dr. Eigil Juel Henningsen from the Ministry of Health. Only certain prisoners were permitted to speak. Those who stood by the road sang and clapped their hands as the delegation passed.

Frants Hvass, Juel Henningsen, and Maurice Rossels concluded their site visit with a report summarizing the favorable conditions of the Danes at Theresienstadt—a brilliant Nazi disguise. Rossels, the Swiss doctor, confirmed the findings of the delegation in his report—Nazi lies. In 1949, Frants Hvass appeared before the Parliamentary Commission and reported that he found that health conditions were better than expected, which was partly due to the agreement enabling food parcels to be sent to the Danish Jews.

Jean-Claude Favez, a historian and member of the ICRC delegation, had a different opinion. He believed that the ICRC knew that exposing the truth and writing a damaging report would have prevented the prisoners from receiving food parcels and postcards.

After the Red Cross left, the Germans felt that the visit had been so successful that they made a propaganda film. After the film was completed, the benches and the children's playground were removed. The Germans convinced the world that Theresienstadt was a model camp. All members of the Ältesterat, who kept their promise not to disclose the actual conditions to the visitors, were sent eastwards to death camps, except for Rabbi Max Friediger.

The Germans prevented the ICRC from seeing the other camps and obtaining the critical information they required. By 1944, the ICRC managed to find out the location of the main concentration camps. Accounts of prisoners who had escaped and other pieces of information reached the organization.

The officers in Theresienstadt allowed us to receive and send strictly censored postcards every six months. We wrote meaningless phrases that satisfied the Gestapo such as "Everything is okay," "Greetings to the family," and "We are healthy and well." Nevertheless, we found methods to convey the truth to the Danish community in Denmark about our hunger and the atrocious conditions of the camp. Our hidden messages were understood in Denmark.

Many of the prisoners would write notes with code words about what they heard at Theresienstadt. They gave the postcards to anyone—civilians, train guards—or simply threw the postcard from the train, hoping that the note would be found. Miraculously, some postcards arrived and confirmed the worst rumors.

During the summer and autumn of 1944, my sister Rebekka's health deteriorated. She was fourteen at the time and suffered again from severe epileptic attacks. Her attacks remained untreated, and her health declined. While we were at work, she spent every day in the shared room with Mrs. Cholewa and the Schwartz couple. Rebekka never recovered.

A turning point in my development was watching the transports leave the camp with thousands of prisoners traveling eastward to the death camps. Every few days, there were trainloads of cattle cars filled with new prisoners. In the autumn of 1944, I was chosen to help prisoners board the trains with their luggage. I saw their pale faces and indescribable expressions, as they knew their fate. The Germans were transporting 1,000 prisoners every three to four days.

The SS officers contacted the Ältesterat and ordered them to select 1,300 prisoners to be transported. After the Nazis gave the order, the Ältesterat gave them lists with names of the "protected" and "unprotected" prisoners. The "protected" ones were Danish Jews and the families of the Ältesterat Jews; the "unprotected" were others. Then the Nazis reduced the number to 1,000 so that each one of the board members could save 30 prisoners

The first two leaders of the Ältesterat, Jacob Edelstein and Paul Epstein, were murdered by the Nazis for not obeying the orders. Dr. Epstein, as previously mentioned, revealed what happened in the East, which led to his demise. Benjamin Murmelstein, who was chairman of the Ältesterat, survived.

The SS officers claimed that the reason for sending the Jews to the death camps was to ease the over-crowded living conditions. By the autumn of 1944, the prisoners and the Ältesterat knew that the Jews were being transported to Auschwitz and other death camps.

One day, as I was helping prisoners board the trains, I suddenly saw the Czech couple. As part of my work duties, I helped them with their luggage.

The husband came up to me and removed his wedding ring. He handed it to me and whispered, "Get me a cigarette." I was startled and desperate. I said, "You can't sell your wedding ring for a cigarette." His answer shocked me as he said, "I don't need it anymore." I ran to the nearest Czech gendarme and sold the beautiful ring for a cigarette. The couple entered the train, and that was the last time I saw them.

In February of 1945, Benjamin Murmelstein received some worrying information about two buildings that were to be built just outside the camp. The Germans ordered us to build two simple buildings about thirty square meters each, constructed with building blocks, without plaster, and one small window. It was to be used as a gas chamber to kill the Jews.

Toward the end, when the Germans realized they were losing the war and the Russians and Allies were approaching, rather than turning the prisoners over to them, they made them walk in treacherous winter conditions. Most of the prisoners died on the way. Jews and non-Jews were forced onto railways cattle cars to be transported outside of Theresienstadt. Some of the prisoners were taken to Poland, and then returned to Theresienstadt. Those that returned to the camp brought sickness, causing thousands of deaths. The original net population of 60,000 prisoners decreased to 19,000.

Many people thought that the rescue of Danish Jews from Theresienstadt was a Swedish initiative under the leadership of Count Folke Bernadotte. But that was incorrect. Count Folke was a Swedish diplomat who had been sent to Berlin to negotiate the release of Scandinavian prisoners of war and others. In 1945, he was the vice president of the Swedish Red Cross and negotiated the release of about 22,000 prisoners from German concentration camps. (After the war, Bernadotte was chosen to be the UN Security Council mediator in the Arab-Israeli conflict of 1947–1948. Bernadotte was a hated figure in Israel. In 1948, he was in Jerusalem for an official visit and was assassinated by a paramilitary Zionist group.)

The British were moving from the west, and the Russians from the east. At the same time, warnings sounded from the Jewish Congress that the Jews in Theresienstadt faced mass slaughter.

On April 8, 1945, in a meeting at the Red Cross camp in Friedrichruhe, Germany, Dr. Johannes Holm asked Count Bernadotte for help to release the Danish Jews in Theresienstadt. This became a high priority for the Danish authority. According to Holm, Folke Bernadotte discussed the plan with General Schellenberg, who claimed that the Germans were agreeable to releasing the Danish Jews. The truth was that Bernadotte was not interested in rescuing the Danish Jews from Theresienstadt.

The Swedish and Danish Red Cross had established a base in Friedrichruhe. From there, the delegation began to pick up prisoners from thirty different camps and bring them to Neuengamme to await final permission from the Germans to leave for Denmark and Sweden. During this time, other prisoners had already been transferred to Neuengamme, and some had even crossed the border into Denmark.

In this difficult situation, the Danish delegates decided, in agreement with the Ministry of Foreign Affairs, that the rescue of the Danish Jews had to be a Danish action. The Danish Jews would be picked up and taken directly from Theresienstadt to Sweden. The reason for the direct route was that the Germans still did not allow mixing Jews with other Aryan prisoners such as Danish policemen, communists, or homosexuals.

The Swedish Red Cross buses used petrol and had good tires, while the Danish Red Cross buses were fueled by wood and had bad tires. In a private meeting with German SS officer Karl Rennau, Holm was able to get his support for the plan to take the Danish Jews from Theresienstadt to Denmark. In return, Rennau requested that he, his wife, and his daughter be granted asylum in Denmark after the war. Bribed with Danish schnapps and food, the leadership of the SS changed its view and permitted the release of the Danish Jews from Theresienstadt.

The captain of the Danish Red Cross camp asked Mr. Falke, the captain of the Swedish Red Cross, if they could use the Swedish buses to rescue the Jews in Theresienstadt. Falke agreed to the request. The joint rescue operation by the Danish government and the Swedish Red Cross was called White Buses.

There were two Swedish drivers for each bus. The rest of the crew was from Denmark. At the last minute, Swedish diplomat Arvid Richert received a telephone call from the Swedish Ministry of Foreign Affairs not to allow the use of the Swedish buses from Friedrishruhe, but Falke replied that he could do nothing, as the buses were already on their way. We had a convoy of 23 Swedish buses, ambulances, six vans, a repair car, a crane car, a special kitchen, two private cars, three motorcycles, and doctors and nurses.

On April 13, 1945, something unexpected happened. The Danish prisoners received a letter that the Nazis had handed to the Ältesterat. I still have that letter to this day. It read: *"You are hereby informed that you are selected for a travel group that will leave Theresienstadt. You will bring your luggage and appear at building Bäckergasse 2 this evening, Friday April 13, 1945, between 20:00 and at the latest 22:00 hours."*

When we arrived at the building, we were told that all the Danish prisoners would be picked up by a fleet of Swedish buses and travel to Sweden. While we waited, a middle-aged Danish-German prisoner, Harry Harbo, entertained us. He played a clown, and the German soldiers laughed with us. The buses did not arrive that night nor the next day. In the meantime, the Danish prisoners formed friendships with the Czech prisoners. The Danish chief rabbi asked the SS officer if he (the rabbi) could perform the wedding ceremony for a Danish and Czech couple. The SS agreed. Thus, the two newlyweds could travel with the Danes, which saved their lives.

On Sunday April 15, 1945, the White Buses finally arrived. Each bus had an armed German soldier. We drove through Germany. The three motorcycles drove in front of the convoy to check that the road was passable. There were curtains on the windows, so we could not look out. While driving on the main road between Prague and Dresden, I peeked carefully behind the curtains and saw that Germany had been completely bombed and was in ruins.

The buses drove with their lights off on roads that were full of potholes. When I peeked out of the window as we drove through Dresden, I saw that the buildings were like skeletons. We heard air raid sirens and Allied aircrafts. The buses were marked with large red crosses on the roof, but this was not a guarantee. For safety, the buses increased their speed as they headed toward the forest.

I had no idea how close we were to the Russian and the Allied forces that were pressing forward toward Berlin, which was only a few kilometers away. All I knew is what I was told that we were on the way to the Danish border and that we would continue to Sweden afterwards. I had no idea why we had been rescued while other European Jews in Theresienstadt remained in the camp.

Later, we were informed that on April 18, 1945, the Allies bombed the Danish Red Cross camp in Friedrichruhe, where several buses were damaged, and the crew were wounded. The Germans used the buses to transport soldiers and war material.

On Tuesday April 17, 1945, we passed the Danish border. Along both sides of the road, Danes were standing and waving the Danish flag. It was unforgettable. They shouted "Hurrah!" and welcomed us home. We opened the windows of the buses, and warm-hearted strangers threw food, sweets, and cigarettes to us. We drove through Jutland and then turned toward Funen. We spent the night at the Munkebjerg School before we continued on to Sweden. As a condition of our release from Theresienstadt, we remained in Sweden until the war was over.

In Odense, we ate our first proper meal, but our usual minimal calorie intake did not allow us to digest the delicious food. Some of us vomited, while others lay down with stomach cramps.

On Wednesday April 18, 1945, the day before my seventeenth birthday, we arrived to Malmö, Sweden. We were placed in quarantine for disinfection and were given new clothes.

Everyone began looking for missing family members. My brother and I looked for our father, Fanny, and Ante. Mrs. Cholewa, with whom we had shared living quarters in Theresienstadt, came to us and said she had just received news from one of her close family members. She told us that our father and brother had drowned on their way to Sweden a year and a half ago.

From Malmö, Salle and I were sent by train to Strängnes (Sweden). In the camp at Strängnes, we slowly got used to the nourishing food and regained our strength. My mother and the two siblings were sent to another camp. Three weeks later, we arrived in Gøteborg, Sweden. After more than a year and a half, I was reunited with my sister Fanny, and three weeks later with my mother, Rebekka, and Mogens. Mother was almost unrecognizable. Her face was gray and shrunken. The grief of losing her husband and son had put her into a state of shock.

Fanny never spoke about her experiences. We didn't know that she had swum ashore and had miraculously rescued herself. It was only sixty-three years later when Fanny and I began to talk about the war that I learned the details of her time in Sweden. After her arrival, the police informed her that they had contacted our uncle David, who lived in the northern part of Sweden. They sent Fanny a railway ticket to visit him, but she decided she needed to regain her strength before she saw him. The Swedish authorities provided her with new shoes and clothes. They also informed our uncle about our father's death. He was close to our father and was stunned after he met Fanny.

After the visit, Fanny returned to Helsingborg and stayed there for about six months. My uncle and his family moved to Göteborg. Later,

Fanny moved to her cousin Selma's home. Selma lived near Uncle David and his family. Fanny began working as a seamstress in a small factory. Every month that she received money from the Danish Consulate, she used it to send food parcels to us in Theresienstadt. She could send a postcard, written in German, once every six months. Fanny wrote faithfully but could not bring herself to tell us that our father and our brother Ante had drowned.

Fanny and the other Danish Jews received the news that Swedish buses had brought prisoners home from the concentration camps.

We were freed on May 4, 1945. After forty-five days in Sweden, we returned to Denmark. In Copenhagen, we stayed with other Danes at the Skovshoved School. After a couple of weeks, we were given an apartment in Sydhavnen by the Ministry of Social Affairs, which established an office to take care of the homes and household effects of imprisoned Danish Jews.

While we were imprisoned in Theresienstadt, our neighbors looted our apartment. Only furniture, some cutlery, and family photos remained. These items were handed over to us when we arrived at our new rental apartment in Scandiagade Street. We had to start from scratch: find new beds, furniture, and begin a new life.

When we moved into the new apartment, my mother collapsed and was immovable. She cried every day for the next six months, and it was impossible to comfort her.

Home in Copenhagen after the war.

Fanny left home and married in the autumn of 1945. She had difficulty finding an apartment in Copenhagen, but with the help of her husband they found one on Jagtvej Street.

My mother's weak condition placed a heavy responsibility on my shoulders. Not by choice but by circumstance, I became head of the household, serving as a substitute father for my three younger siblings. This created a heavy burden when I was still reeling after the war, trying to cope with the memory of the terrible things I had witnessed and experienced.

Mogens was seven years old and had to start school. Salle became an apprentice shoemaker. Rebekka, who was now thirteen, had not received any treatment for her epilepsy while living in the camps, so I had to take her to a special hospital far from Copenhagen for treatment. She was placed in a room with an elderly woman who cried and screamed all the time. Rebekka had violent cramps, lost consciousness, and her face became swollen. We always had to make sure that she didn't bite her tongue. Finally, her situation improved, and she was released from the hospital. Then she started to work.

My mother received a monthly payment from the Danish government. We urgently needed support from a social worker, but that did not exist at that time. I had no connection with any government office, so I had to deal with all our family problems myself for four years.

During the first six months in Denmark, my mother tried to commit suicide twice. One day after returning home from school, I smelled gas coming from the apartment. I knew that I shouldn't ring the bell because it could cause an explosion. I opened the door and saw my mother sitting in a chair. All the windows were closed, and the gas valves were fully open. I ran to the kitchen stove to close the taps, and then opened the windows. I dragged my mother to one of the open windows. I could not trust her to take care of herself. A short time later, she made another suicide attempt.

In those years, our family, like most other Jewish families, were stricken with grief over the life they had dreamt of and that disappeared. At home, we never spoke about our tragedies.

When Rebekka was nineteen, she swallowed a large number of sleeping pills. I found her lying in bed with pale skin and a big pillbox next to her. I called an ambulance. In the hospital, the medics pumped her stomach, and the doctor sent her home. The next morning, I went into her room to see how she was doing. She was lying in bed; her eyes were closed, and she looked calm and relaxed. She was dead. I never discovered the reason for her suicide. She died on November 20, 1951, a short time before her twentieth birthday. My mother, who had lost so much in her life, suffered yet another severe blow.

In the summer of 1949, while I was on a bicycle tour with a friend, I met Birgit at a youth hostel in the Danish town of Vejle. Birgit was with her girlfriend Hanna Posner and Hanna's younger brother. Birgit and I began to see each other at Jewish youth clubs and on other occasions. Birgit lived in Vanløse.

After returning to Denmark from Theresienstadt, I was only seventeen-years old, and lost two years of school. I re-enrolled in school to continue my education studying two years, obtaining my middle school diploma.

After five years, Birgit and I got engaged on New Year's Eve 1950. I began to study at Denmark's Technical High School. While a student, I helped my uncle at his butcher shop and worked sorting mail at the central post office in Copenhagen. Due to economic reasons, Birgit and I decided to get married after I finished my studies.

Birgit and I were married on November 28, 1954, between two examinations and just three months before my final engineering examination. We were given an apartment for which only married couples were eligible. In February of 1955 I passed my final examination, and a new era began.

Robert and Birgit married in Denmark.

During the summer of 1955, Birgit and I took our first trip abroad and traveled to Germany with friends. On June 12, 1957, our first daughter, Rina, was born. At about the same time, we bought a plot of land in Skovlunde, where I built a twenty-square-meter summer house. Our second daughter, Ora, was born on March 6, 1960.

In 1964, Birgit and I decided to go to Israel for one year to live on a kibbutz. We wanted to better understand the Israeli culture and society to decide if becoming Israeli citizens would be the best decision for our family. To get to the ship that would take us to Israel, we drove through Eastern Europe to Piraeus, Greece. Our route took us through East Germany, Czechoslovakia, Yugoslavia, and Greece. We rented our house to the American director of an oil company.

On September 16, 1964, we sailed from Piraeus to Haifa. We then made our way to Kibbutz Gal'ed, situated south of the Carmel Mountains. The kibbutz was founded in 1948, mainly by German Jews. While on the kibbutz, we attended an intensive Hebrew class for four hours per day and worked for another four hours. At first, our daughters, aged four and seven, lived with us. Later, they were moved to the children's houses.

Life in the kibbutz was different than what we had imagined. After five months, one month before our six-month commitment was up, we left the kibbutz because I found a job as an engineer in Tel Aviv. We moved to Ramat Hasharon, north of Tel Aviv. My mother came to visit us and met her cousins from Poland who had emigrated to Israel in the 1950s. They were pale, thin, and nervous. They sat still and spoke about their time in Nazi concentration camps.

We returned to Denmark in 1965. I worked as an engineer for Krone and Koch, a large well-respected company that provided annual salary increases. We bought a dog, spent time at our summer house, and went on vacations abroad. Birgit became chairwoman of the International Women's Zionist Help Organization in Denmark.

In 1972, after I had accumulated many hours of overtime at my job, Birgit suggested that I go to Israel for a short visit and stay with her family there. During my brief visit, I interviewed with three companies, and each offered me a position. Hadassah hospital in Jerusalem was the most preferable because of my prior work experience in hospital installations. The salary was much less than I earned in Denmark, but to compensate for the difference, Hadassah would provide my family with health insurance and a provisional apartment. Two weeks later, when I was back in Denmark, they offered me a three-year contract. The hospital wanted me to begin work immediately, so I decided to go to Israel while Birgit and Ora remained in Denmark until our house was sold.

My biggest dilemma was leaving my mother in Denmark. I returned from Israel on a Thursday, and four days later Birgit and I went to the Israeli immigration authorities to sign immigration papers to make aliya.

While we were living in Israel, I visited our families at least once or twice each year. In 1972, Birgit came to Israel with Ora to sign a contract to purchase an apartment in the French Hill neighborhood of Jerusalem, through the Jewish Agency. We lived there for 19 years. After the transaction was completed, Birgit returned to Denmark to complete the sale of our home. Ora remained in Israel. After completing my three-year contract with Hadassah, I went to work as a private engineer for the Hebrew University of Jerusalem.

During the Yom Kippur War in 1973, I volunteered as a driver for the Israeli army to bring soldiers from Jericho to Jerusalem and vice versa. In addition, I helped to maintain the machines at the largest bakery in Jerusalem when the regular staff was called up for army duty.

Birgit worked as a volunteer for the army and at one of the archaeological museums in Jerusalem. We heard there was an urgent need for Scandinavian tour guides. Birgit decided to become a professional tour guide, so she took an eighteen-month course offered by the Ministry of Tourism. From time to time, she went on excursions in Israel that lasted seven to ten days.

With Birgit's periodic trips away, I decided to leave my engineering profession and become a licensed tour guide as well so that we could spend more time together. At that time, there was a great demand for tour guides who spoke Scandinavian languages and German. Birgit and I worked as Israeli tour guides for thirty years, traveling throughout Israel and abroad, visiting more than thirty countries.

After living in French Hill, we purchased a plot of land in Tzur Hadassah, just outside of Jerusalem, and built a new home. We lived there for over twenty-two years. The home was exquisite. Tzur Hadassah, which was once a moshav, was later converted into a small housing community. In 2015, we moved to an apartment in Kfar Saba, where we live today.

My mother remained in Denmark and died at the age of eighty-two. Mogens is married and lives in Denmark with three children and grandchildren. I have a good relationship with his grandson, an established photojournalist. Salle is now ninety years old and still lives in Denmark. He has two children and three grandchildren. Fanny, a widow, died and had two children and grandchildren.

I am blessed with two children, eight grandchildren, and seven great-grandchildren. On November 28, 2019, Birgit and I celebrated our sixty-fifth wedding anniversary, but really, we have been together for seventy years.

Robert's daughter Solveig Rina and her husband Dani.

Robert and Birgit.

Further Reading

Beit Hatfutsot The Museum of the Jewish People, Open Databases Project, https://dbs.bh.org.il
Leo Baeck Institute, https://www.lbi.org
Jewish Archives of Bukovina and Transylvania, https://jbat.lbi.org
Yad Vashem, The World Holocaust Research Center
Digital Collections, https://www.yadvashem.org/collections.html
The Untold Stories database, https://www.yadvashem.org/untoldstories/database/homepage.asphttps://www.yadvashem.org/untoldstories/database/homepage.asp
Yivo Institute for Jewish Research, https://www.yivo.org
Yivo Encyclopedia of Jews in Eastern Europe, https://yivoencyclopedia.org/default.aspx

Târgu Mureş
https://www.encyclopedia.com/religion/encyclopedias-almanacs-transcripts-and-maps/targu-mures
https://dbs.bh.org.il/place/targu-mures

Transylvania
https://www.britannica.com/place/Transylvania
https://yivoencyclopedia.org/article.aspx/Transylvania

Dr. Miklós Nyiszli
http://www.auschwitz.dk/Nyiszli.htm
https://www.ncbi.nlm.nih.gov/pmc/articles/PMC4374105/
https://www.imdb.com/name/nm0638699/bio

Burdujeni
https://www.jewishgen.org/communities/community.php?usbgn=-1154220
https://jbat.lbi.org/locality/burdujeni
https://www.jewishvirtuallibrary.org/burdujeni

Suceava
https://dbs.bh.org.il/place/suceava

Rovno
https://yivoencyclopedia.org/article.aspx/Rivne https://www.encyclopedia.com/religion/encyclopedias-almanacs-transcripts-and-maps/rovno

Warkowicze
https://www.yadvashem.org/untoldstories/database/index.asp?cid=1110
Kiskunmajsa
https://dbs.bh.org.il/place/kiskunmajsa

Kiskunhalas
https://dbs.bh.org.il/place/hajdunanas

Hajdúnánás
https://dbs.bh.org.il/place/hajdunanas

Index

About The Author

I was born and raised in San Francisco, California. I moved to Israel on February 21, 1993. I married my wife Emanuela, who is from Rome, Italy, in 1995. We have four children: Yonathan, Danielle, Ben, and Roy. Since 1995, we have been living in Ra'anana, Israel.

This is my first book. My next one, which is half complete, is about the untold stories of the rich Middle Eastern cuisines in Israel, against their historical background dating back 3,000 years. I unearthed close to thirty of the best restaurants in Israel representing Middle Eastern and Balkan cuisines. These underground authentic eateries, truly "off the road" family run, offer rich authentic dishes from family recipes passed down through generations, which they are now sharing with the public together with details of their personal histories. The book will have essays about the history of Jews from each country, including Bedouins, Druze and Circassians, contributed by historians and professors.

When the global COVID-19 pandemic is resolved, I intend to concentrate my writing on the lives of Jews from the "12 Lost Tribes." One book on the horizon will be about the little known but historic wealth of Jewish culture and history of the Bnei Menashe tribe, who reside in India's northeastern states of Mizoram and Manipur on the border of Myanmar. This lost Jewish tribe, now recognized by the State of Israel as Jews, converted to Christianity prior to the nineteenth century.

www.ingramcontent.com/pod-product-compliance
Lightning Source LLC
Chambersburg PA
CBHW021507090426
42739CB00007B/499